Standing with Stones

with

RUPERT SOSKIN

Standing
with **Stones**

A Photographic Journey Through
Megalithic Britain & Ireland

Foreword by Timothy Darvill

with 248 photographs

Thames & Hudson

To my wife Julie
and my sons Damien and Alex

Endpapers: *Yellowmead in Devon.*
Half-title: *A Bronze Age cist near Drizzlecombe, Dartmoor.*
Title page: *Isle of Lewis – Callanish in silhouette.*

Photograph page 64, below, copyright English Heritage.

First published in the United Kingdom in 2009
by Thames & Hudson Ltd, 181A High Holborn, London WC1V 7QX

www.thamesandhudson.com

© 2009 Rupert Soskin

Foreword © 2009 Timothy Darvill

The right of Rupert Soskin to be identified as author of the work
has been asserted by him in accordance with the Copyright, Design
and Patents Act 1998

British Library Cataloguing-in-Publication Data
A catalogue record for this book is available from the British Library

ISBN 978-0-500-05158-0

Printed in China by Hing Yip Printing Co. Ltd.

FOREWORD

Stonehenge rocks! This is the catch-phrase printed on the latest range of merchandise available at Europe's most famous prehistoric monument. And it certainly does, with streams of visitors ambling around the perimeter path gazing at the jumbled stones inside and continuing an age-old fascination with megaliths. Beyond Stonehenge there are literally thousands of other stone monuments of the Neolithic and Bronze Age awaiting attention. In this captivating book Rupert Soskin introduces a selection of them, some easy of access but others remote and isolated in their abandonment. Always, as he gently shows, there are many different ways of seeing them. Modern scientific archaeology tends to focus on the materials used, how they were built and the date of construction. But just as important are the visual and aesthetic qualities so well captured by Rupert's stunning and original photographs. These act like windows into the past, encouraging us to think more widely about the meaning and purpose of ancient sites, how they were perceived by prehistoric people, and at the same time opening the eyes of travellers and enthusiasts to the great wealth and variety of standing stones across the British Isles.

Timothy Darvill
Professor of Archaeology
Centre for Archaeology, Anthropology and Heritage
Bournemouth University, UK

CONTENTS

LAND'S END TO ORKNEY

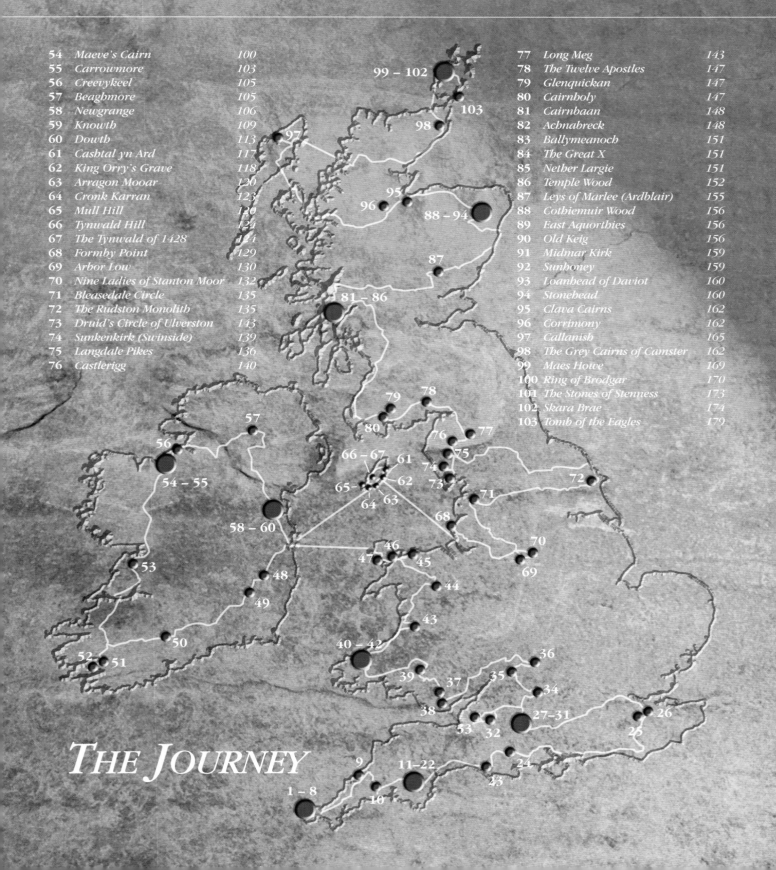

THE JOURNEY

Above: Cornwall's enormous Trethevy Quoit.
Opposite: Sunrise at Callanish on the Hebridean island of Lewis.

So Much We Have Forgotten

Have you ever wondered why a 5,000-year-old standing stone can rise proud of the landscape when buildings more recent than the Romans may have sunk six feet into the ground? Or why so many stone circles had nineteen stones? Chances are that you either already know the answers, or you never knew the questions were there to be asked. Whichever applies, whether you are an avid explorer of Britain's prehistoric monuments or simply enjoy the occasional visit to mysterious sites encountered on your travels, most readers will share a wonder and a fascination for the tantalizing remains of our ancestors' seemingly alien lives.

Imagine that our present-day architecture could stand the test of time, and 5,000 years in the future our descendants begin excavating the empty shells of our buildings. There would be nothing to show them the difference between a hospital and an office block, a warehouse store and an aircraft hangar, or even a church hall and a jazz club. Very often, the imposing megalithic structures of our ancestors present precisely this problem. For example, when is a stone circle just a circle of stones, and why might it be important to know the difference? Because you often find that people have tied prayer ribbons around what probably used to be a pig pen. Obviously I'm not diminishing the value of livestock here, but it is a simple mistake if one is only looking for circles of stone and believing them all to be sacred.

Having spent many years exploring the wealth of ancient sites across the British Isles, I have often been surprised (and quietly pleased) to have them entirely to myself. But even if we prefer experiencing these places in solitude, we still enjoy sharing our thoughts and comparing notes with others who have visited the same and other monuments at different times. But how many ancient monuments are widely known? Ask someone at random in the street to name half a dozen megalithic sites. The first answer is invariably Stonehenge, followed after a few seconds by Avebury and perhaps Silbury Hill, then the pauses grow longer as people grope for names they may hardly even have known. Tourists may offer Newgrange in Ireland, or the Rollright Stones in Oxfordshire, but it is often only people already interested in the subject or locals who will know even the mightiest sites such as Callanish in the Hebrides, Castlerigg in Cumbria, or Cornwall's Trethevy Quoit.

Again, when asked to estimate the number of stone circles across the British Isles, the correct answer of over a thousand is usually met with total astonishment. If you include all the cairns, henges, barrows, cists, stone rows, dolmens and standing stones as well, a guess at the overall number of prehistoric sites throughout the islands probably becomes pointless.

Above: Shadows creep across Cumbria's Castlerigg in the evening light.
Opposite below: Cornwall's elegant Chun Quoit.
Below: Sunlight illuminates the chamber of Maes Howe, Orkney.

In 2005 I began work on a documentary film, also called *Standing with Stones*, taking a journey through megalithic Britain and Ireland. At the time, my personal estimate for the British Isles was around 50,000 sites in total, but whilst researching in Ireland, I was dumbfounded to discover that there are over 5,000 listed archaeological sites in County Sligo alone. The number does include more recent monuments, but I gave up guessing at that point, largely in fear of becoming a type of obsessional megalithic train spotter.

Misunderstandings about our ancestors can be frustratingly enduring. Even today it is not uncommon to visit sites with information boards depicting Neolithic and Bronze Age people wearing skins and referring to them as farming folk. Certainly they farmed, but the wealth of sophisticated artifacts and monuments tells us that their existence was anything but basic. We also know from the presence of common building characteristics and tools that our distant ancestors shared knowledge and traded over huge distances, yet the image of a simple and insular people lingers in popular imagination.

Much of my time for the last thirty years or so has been spent researching natural sciences, in particular evolutionary psychology, natural history, geology and archaeology. The making of *Standing with Stones*, both film and book, has been a voyage of discovery which altered my own perceptions of prehistory immeasurably. Tantalizing signs of life give way to intimate signs of lives, sometimes so familiar that our ancestors cannot fail to come alive in the imagination. Like walking in Neolithic footprints at Formby Point, or standing in front of a dresser at Skara Brae, knowing that it is the same spot where its owner must so many times have stood ... suddenly it's personal.

As a form of detective work, the task of picking out ancient cultural characteristics is enthralling, and many archaeologists do a fabulous job. The drawing together of clues from hundreds of sites creates a rich and exciting picture. Perhaps our dry image of the past has much to do with the attitudes of the earlier archaeologists? How anyone could explore the sheer artistry, magic and genius of Scotland's many lunar-

Above: The vast Stanton Drew in Somerset is the second largest stone circle in Britain.
Opposite below: Neolithic footprints at Formby Point in Merseyside.
Below: Cothiemuir Wood, a fine example of a 'How did they do this without pen, paper and sextant?' stone circle.

celebrating monuments and call them 'recumbent stone circles' is beyond me. Even *'How did they do this without pen, paper and sextant?'* stone circles would seem more appropriate.

Culturally, our Neolithic and Bronze Age ancestors may appear to have been primitive in comparison with modern society, but in evolutionary terms we are essentially the same. We spend so much time obsessing about their spiritual practices that a rounded view of their world seldom has the chance to arise. For example, when does anybody mention games or other leisure pursuits? These people had the time to be creative. Items such as elaborate works of art and decorated pottery show that they had subsistence sufficiently under control to be able to dedicate time to unessential activities. There is plenty of evidence for ritual and feasting on a grand scale, but what other social activities took place within these societies? And how much interaction took place *between* different social groups?

It is important to remember that our modern cities are the highly developed faces of settlements established all those years ago. Whether for religious or practical reasons, it is because the more recent conurbations where most of us live have erased nearly all trace of any ancient monuments lying beneath that we came to lose our links with the past. This makes it all the more magical to find direct connections with our forebears. The remains of Neolithic and Bronze Age graves in a number of churchyards around Britain tell us that, even today, we still place our dead in the burial grounds chosen by our ancestors. King Orry's Grave on the Isle of Man, the villages surrounding Knocknarea in Ireland and numerous sites across England show that there has been unbroken human habitation for thousands of years, whilst research into regional folklore often reveals the possible traces of something real, something tangible, from a time so distant we believed it forgotten.

Above: The town of Strandhill at the foot of Knocknarea, the modern face of an ancient settlement.
Opposite below: Rudston – a Bronze Age grave lies in the corner of the Christian graveyard.
Below: Some sites, especially on open moorlands, are almost impossible to find without a good map or GPS unit.

The purpose of this book is to share photographically the wonder and beauty of our enigmatic prehistoric sites, and to explore some of the questions which somehow never seem to be addressed outside academic circles. The book is divided into regions, from south to north, with the Ordnance Survey grid reference for each site to assist the would-be visitor. Measurements, where relevant, are imperial. As Colin Ridler of Thames & Hudson put it: 'Old measurements for old stones'.

Anyone with an interest in the subject will appreciate just how awesome and beautiful these places can be. Even the magical surroundings where they so often lie hidden can make a visit worthwhile. So if any of the photographs within these pages make you want to get out the map and put on your walking boots, this book will have done its job.

the
southwest

Carn Gluze,
the Ballowall Barrow

SW355313

Beginning a journey through megalithic Britain in the far south of Cornwall, any explorer would be forgiven for expecting a taste of things to come. But situated high on the cliffs overlooking the sea near Land's End, Carn Gluze, also known as the Ballowall Barrow, is a site unlike any other in the whole of the British Isles.

Structurally, Carn Gluze is a multi-phase round cairn consisting of a central mound encircled by a broad stone platform which in its day would probably have formed an unbroken surface reaching the edge of the raised section. The site incorporates a number of cists, ritual pits and an entrance grave. Much of its reconstruction was carried out by William Borlase, who excavated the site in the 1870s when it was covered, and ironically protected by waste from the nearby tin mine. His work made its appearance somewhat more confusing, but Borlase did at least achieve his intention of making the internal features more clearly visible to visitors.

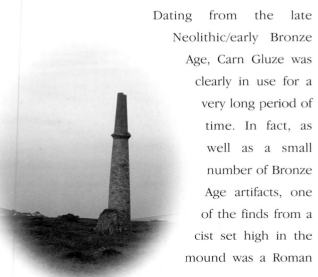

Dating from the late Neolithic/early Bronze Age, Carn Gluze was clearly in use for a very long period of time. In fact, as well as a small number of Bronze Age artifacts, one of the finds from a cist set high in the mound was a Roman coin, which could imply an even longer period of social importance. Of course, it is always possible that this is nothing more than an example of the common practice continued today of leaving personal tokens at ancient and sacred sites. Although the individual features of Carn Gluze are common to many prehistoric sites, as a whole it is an enigma. Perhaps the lesson to learn from this extraordinary site is always to expect the unexpected.

Above: A view over Carn Gluze to the southwest, with one of the pits excavated by William Borlase visible in the foreground.
Opposite: The ruin of the nearby tin mine makes a useful landmark, but also raises the question of how much surrounding archaeology has been destroyed.
Right: Artist's impression of how Carn Gluze may have looked in its Bronze Age form.

Above: The circle of Boscawen-Un.
Both Tregeseal's Dancing Stones (opposite below) and the Merry Maidens (below)
derive their names from early Christian superstition.

Boscawen-Un, Tregeseal & the Merry Maidens

SW412274, SW386324 & SW433245

An interesting characteristic of many West Country stone circles is that they have nineteen stones, and these three fine examples stand close to each other not far from Cornwall's Land's End. Whilst there is no direct evidence, it does seem likely that these rings were built to follow the moon's 18.61-year cycle. Boscawen-Un, a mile north of St Buryan, is one of the finest. It is unusual in having a central monolith which leans at such a low angle it was thought to have sunk to its present position. Surprisingly, however, excavations showed it to have been carefully placed and possibly angled towards the midsummer sunrise.

Three and a half miles north-northwest of Boscawen-Un, out on the open moors of Truthwall Common, Tregeseal is the last surviving stone circle of a close-set group of three which were aligned on an east–west axis. It is also almost all that remains of a once vast settlement. Also known as the Dancing Stones, its name shares the same quaint origin as another of these circles, the Merry Maidens, just over two miles south-southeast of Boscawen-Un.

Myth has it that they were all young maidens turned to stone for dancing on the sabbath. The area around the Merry Maidens is rich in megaliths. On the other side of the road from the circle is a holed stone, long since moved from its original position to become a gate post. Just down the road, the chambered tomb of Tregiffian bears some splendid cupmarks and a short walk away are two huge standing stones known as the Pipers, musicians turned to stone for foolishly accompanying the same unfortunate maidens.

Above: Looking northwest from beneath the stones of Lanyon Quoit.
Below: Chun is one of the smaller Cornish quoits.
Opposite: The enormous Trethevy Quoit.

Lanyon, Chun & Trethevy Quoits

SW430337, SW402340 & SX259688

When is a dolmen not a dolmen? When it's a quoit or a cromlech. In the West Country, these Neolithic portal tombs vary greatly in size and, it has to be said, air of stability. Despite being largely reconstructed in the nineteenth century, Lanyon Quoit looks as if the stones haven't shifted since the day it was erected. Chun, on the other hand, gives the impression of a slowly collapsing house of cards. Trethevy is a mighty construction, with its precarious-looking capstone seeming to defy gravity and its sheer size lending it a sense of immortality. Each of these three were built on stone mounds, and whilst many dolmens were buried beneath earth and stone cairns, Trethevy and Chun at least were never completely covered, as if concealing them would somehow do the stones an injustice.

For the visitor these sites couldn't be more different. Lanyon stands close to the road on level farmland and Trethevy's neighbours are the nearby houses just the other side of the lane. Chun, however, stands proud but discreet on high ground not far from the impressive site of Chun Castle. The castle remains are later, dating from the Iron Age, showing us clearly that these empty lands were home to many for a very, very long time.

Opposite and above: The unique arrangement of stones at Men An Tol.
Below: Field walls nearby are full of large stones which could have
been robbed from the settlement surrounding the site.

Men An Tol *SW426349*

There are so many theories and so few facts about this megalithic mystery. Men An Tol is usually attributed to the Bronze Age, but its true age is far from certain. The unique arrangement of stones has secured a lasting, and unusually interactive, place in local folklore. Passing through the central stone ring has long been said to cure a host of ailments from rickets to tuberculosis; it was even said to aid fertility. But myths aside, it is almost all that remains of a much larger site. Archaeologists uncovered the remains of a stone circle encompassing the mysterious formation. The field boundary walls in all directions are lined with large stones that look as if they could originally have come from the structure and its surrounding settlement.

Men An Tol sits on low and open farmland within easy reach of many other megalithic wonders. But despite the theories of sun alignments, temple or burial site, this prehistoric monument probably remains the most enigmatic of all.

Above and opposite: Despite the name, the number of stones in the Nine Maidens circle has changed many times over the centuries.
Below: A Bronze Age maze carving at Rocky Valley.

The Nine Maidens & Rocky Valley
SW435351 & SX073895

Not far to the east of Men An Tol, the Nine Maidens, also known as Boskednan, is fairly forlorn as circles go. Despite its name, originally the ring was probably another group of nineteen, but as with so many sites, over the centuries stones have been hauled away to lie anonymously in farm walls. A history of robbing, collapse and more recent restoration has taken the standing survivors from their original number to as few as six and currently up to eleven. Perhaps one day we will see the group the way they once were.

Further east, sounding like a far away place from a European fairy tale, Rocky Valley lies hidden in the craggy cliffs between Tintagel and Boscastle. Following the path inland from the shore, it would be easy to miss a pair of Bronze Age maze carvings cut low on a rock face behind the ruins of an old mill. At first glance these mystical carvings seem simple, but tracing a finger through either maze reveals them to be a sophisticated design made of a single line. Even hidden away in places such as this with little else to see, our ancestors left signs that their lives were so much richer and more complex than we sometimes imagine.

Fernworthy & Froggymead   *SX662834 & SX654841*

The area to the west of Fernworthy Reservoir on Dartmoor, Devon, is almost overflowing with standing stones, cairns, stone rows and hut circles. A number of these sites are hard to find, so an OS map or GPS is essential. One unnamed circle lies close to a sharp bend in the road which runs through the forestry plantation. Of the great many hut circles on Dartmoor, this is unusually solid in construction. More significantly, within the circle there is a stone with five carefully cut slots on its upper surface. These slots are generally considered to have been cut much more recently, to make gateposts from conveniently available raw material. An identical stone, probably from one of the nearby circles, has indeed become a gatepost by the car parking area at the end of the road, though its slots are unused and face the wrong way. I know of another such stone, identical in every way and set in approximately the same position within its circle, which, perhaps surprisingly is in the east of Ireland, at a site called Castleruddery (see page 94). I have to say, that whilst they clearly could be unfinished gateposts, their positioning and matching number of slots, plus the absence of examples where the slots are actually used, makes me question this interpretation.

A little over half a mile from the hut circle, to the right of the track, lies the ritual centre of the surrounding monuments. The Fernworthy Circle, also rather quaintly known as Froggymead (no doubt after its amphibian-friendly location), is a ring comprised of small stones which give a misleading impression of simplicity. The site as a whole, however, is a complex affair.

Avenues of small stones radiating out to the north, south and east lead to a number of cairns, cists and mounds which are now all but impossible to photograph amidst the dense undergrowth. However, photographs from the early 1900s show the circle on a treeless moor, before the post-war plantation concealed its relationship with the Grey Wethers double ring (page 45), little over a mile to the southwest. Aubrey Burl records that when the site was excavated in 1897, the Froggymead ring was found to be full of charcoal fragments. Interestingly, both of the Grey Wethers circles revealed exactly the same practice, most probably relating to funerary rites or ceremonies.

From an archaeological point of view, the plantation is at best an encumbrance, but to the megalith hunter, every clearing can hold an unexpected surprise. It would take days fully to explore this small patch of Dartmoor, and it is worth bearing in mind that not all these monuments are individually marked on even the best maps. Astonishingly, there are over 1,200 protected ancient monuments on the moor, too many of them forgotten and unnamed.

Assycombe *SX661826*

Standing in the southern section of the Fernworthy plantation is one of my favourite of all Dartmoor's monuments. The stone row at Assycombe seems to be bursting out of the hillside like the spine of an emerging giant reptile.

An imposing monolith or blocking stone stands at the head of the avenue, which leads down to a hut circle on the left at the bottom of the hill. A little searching soon reveals more hut circles in the nearby clearings. This whole area is just plain busy, and was clearly the centre of a great deal of Bronze Age activity.

The largest, called the Giant's Basin, has fallen in on itself, significantly reducing its height, but it remains, nonetheless, imposing.

Continuing east, the remains of settlements, cairns, cists and circles cover the landscape, stretching beyond the south side of the improbably named Higher Hartor Tor. At the eastern edge of the group is a well-preserved cairn circle with central cist known as Grim's Grave, and heading northeast from here, back towards Higher Hartor Tor, the prehistoric remains stretch on and on, seemingly countless. Many of the cists have lost their capstones, so the sunken stone boxes are often hidden in the grass, popping into view unexpectedly or tripping up the unwary walker.

The local place names often seem strange, but none more so than the sinister-sounding Evil Combe, a deep and gloomy valley behind Higher Hartor Tor. It is perhaps a relief to find that the name has nothing to do with Satanic witchcraft or ritual sacrifice, but relates to the region's more recent past. Interestingly, if slightly disappointing, an 'evel' was a four-pronged fork used by the field workers. The truth will out, but the later misspelling makes for a much more enthralling landscape.

Right: The well-preserved cairn circle known as Grim's Grave at grid reference SX612663.

Left: Looking southwest along one of the Drizzlecombe stone rows.

Above and opposite: Views east and west along Merrivale's impressive stone rows.
Below: The tall outlier close to the southern stone circle.

Merrivale SX555747

It is perhaps an irony that Dartmoor's astonishing wealth of megalithic monuments remains intact because our ancestors began to clear the dense forest which once covered the landscape. Thousands of years of deforestation made the land increasingly inhospitable and infertile, which, coupled with slow climate change, ultimately left huge areas suitable only for grazing. Had the trees remained to shed their leaves, the soil would have been enriched, and over time, engulfed the sites, as we see in so many other parts of Britain. This is all the more apparent at Merrivale, where dozens upon dozens of Bronze Age structures stand on a level plain, easily visible, but still requiring more than a single visit to explore them all.

The site extends both north and south of the road, the main part of the complex being on the southern side. The complex is dominated by two imposing double stone rows, but as well as a smaller single row, the site also contains two stone circles, many hut circles, and numerous cairns and cists. The southern stone circle is the more elegant of the two. The stones of the ring itself are all small, but this only serves to draw attention to the tall monolith which stands over them. It is easy to be so captivated by Merrivale's rows that the hut circles closer to the road can be overlooked. To me this is a shame. Beyond death and ritual, these are the structures which connect us to our ancestors' daily lives.

Opposite: Looking north along one of Shovel Down's stone rows.
Remains of the multiple-ringed circle can be seen in the foreground.
Above: The northern arc of the Scorhill stone circle.
Below: Scorhill from the higher ground to the northeast.

Shovel Down & Scorhill SX659860 & SX654873

There are a number of ways to reach the Scorhill stone circle but none more rewarding than the walk from Batworthy across Shovel Down. It is a magical experience, when visiting ancient sites, to realize that we are sharing a space where our ancestors once stood, and even more magical when one considers just how long ago that was. Shovel Down has given up prehistoric remains dating back to the Mesolithic, perhaps older than 10,000 years ago, when almost all of Dartmoor was still covered in dense forest. The stone rows and monoliths we see today date from around 4,000 years ago, and looking carefully across the landscape, a keen eye will pick out the long, low banks of ancient field boundaries. The tired remains of a multiple-ringed circle, like that at Yellowmead (page 34), stand somewhat forlornly at the top of the northern row.

Beyond this complex and jumbled settlement, the stones of Scorhill can be seen on the opposite hillside. The path leads to a pretty clapper bridge which crosses the stream at the bottom of the valley and the circle itself, despite having been robbed of many of its stones, remains a truly splendid sight.

*Above: The remains of a stone structure inside Kraps Ring. The surrounding low bank
is just visible as a darker green band rising from the long grass.
Opposite and below: Unusually large cists punctuate the complex to the south of the ring.*

Kraps Ring SX644782

The Kraps Ring settlement lies on the north side of Lakehead Hill, but the full complex extends all the way to Bellever Tor a mile to the south. It was a bitterly cold winter day when I first visited the site and seldom have I been so thawed by the wonder of a place; these people did nothing by halves. Kraps Ring itself is defined by a low and rather modest bank, creating a large irregular circle, flattened on its southern edge. Walking out of the ring to the south, however, all sense of modesty disappears. Stone rows lead to cairn circles with some of the largest cists on the moor. This group of monuments is grand.

It is interesting to contrast the characteristics of this site with others such as Drizzlecombe (page 34), where enormous rows lead to small cists. Here, the rows are short and the graves themselves are much larger, as if the funeral procession was a less important aspect of the ceremonial than the burials themselves. The shorter rows could also imply processions of fewer people, perhaps just priests or nobles, and it is tempting to wonder whether burials like this were more private rituals, reserved solely for the community's elite.

Above: The massive Round Pound is essentially a prehistoric small holding.
Opposite below: The pretty cairn circle of Giant's Grave is the easiest of the group to find.
Below: The enormous double circle of Grey Wethers viewed from the slopes of Sittaford Tor.

Round Pound, Grey Wethers & Giant's Grave

SX664868, SX639832 & SX767877

To the side of the road not far from Shovel Down, Round Pound is a massive construction, the largest of a once sizeable group of similar structures. Excavations in the 1950s appear to show that it was in continuous use from the Bronze Age right through the Iron Age and possibly even until medieval times. Here a large hut circle sits within a wide, circular pound. This outer circle would have held livestock, and it remained common practice until fairly recently to live in extremely close proximity to your animals. In total contrast, the Grey Wethers double circle is a vast Bronze Age ceremonial site, one of the largest on Dartmoor, and it has been suggested that it may have been a meeting place for clans from different parts of the moor. Certainly, it is worth the long walk; approaching from any direction reveals countless monuments along the way.

Six miles from the moor, close to Mardon Down, a small group, collectively marked on maps as Giant's Grave, stretches in a north–south line over the brow of a gentle hill with clear views across the surrounding countryside. The site contains a number of cairns, a stone circle and a cairn circle – in other words a ceremonial circle and a burial circle. Apart from the cairn circle, it can become so overgrown that sometimes, hunting out these pretty but unimposing monuments can bring needle and haystack to mind.

45

the south

Opposite and below: Moss makes this tiny stone appear to blend seamlessly into the beech tree which cradles it.
Above: The stones' massively contrasting heights give the larger ones an even greater dominance.

Nine Stones SY611904

Just a few miles west of Dorchester in Dorset, this little Bronze Age circle stands quietly by the side of the A35, all but ignored by the passing traveller. The circle is about thirty feet across at its widest and this small arrangement is echoed in its predominantly tiny stones. However, these only serve to make the two huge stones closest to the road seem even more powerful, like stern parents standing over expectant children. A cursory glance at the map shows the surrounding area to be full of largely inaccessible prehistoric remains, mostly tumuli, as well as a few circles and long barrows. There are over two hundred sites within a five-mile radius, showing just how lively this region must have been a few thousand years ago.

On the south side of the circle, a beautiful mature beech has wrapped its roots around one of the smaller stones. In a way it adds to the sense of overall neglect, but at the same time puts our own existence into perspective, considering that the tree's two or three human lifespans pale into insignificance next to the age of the circle it has attempted to join. Be warned: the A35 is busy and this stretch is flanked by drainage ditches. Park with care and run like hell!

The Chestnuts & Coldrum

TQ653592 & TQ654607

The massive Neolithic long barrow at the Chestnuts in Addington, Kent, is a good indication of how, throughout history, land has been divided into progressively smaller and smaller plots. This magnificent site now lies hidden away in a private garden, separated from other ancient remains by the surrounding lanes and hedges. Its fallen capstone leans against another stone, which it appears to have knocked over when it fell. The long barrow itself remains an awesome sight; certainly no lover of megaliths could wish for a better garden feature.

Less than a mile to the north are the remains of another Neolithic long barrow, so different in appearance that the contrast alone makes them worth the visit. Coldrum sits on a high mound with clear, sweeping views down through the Medway Valley. Most of the original structure has long since disappeared, but the bulky stones of the burial chamber still dominate the site, seeming to balance precariously on the eastern edge of the mound. A number of other stones have tumbled to the foot of the slope, making it even harder to imagine how it must have looked all those thousands of years ago.

Excavations at Coldrum uncovered the bones of over twenty people. Possibly the most interesting was a skull

thought to be of an adult female, who had been killed by the blow of a stone axe to the back of the head. Whether this was murder or sacrifice is unknown, but even though it is a reminder of death, this kind of discovery can bring a place to life.

Above: The Chestnuts long barrow.
Opposite and right: Views from the top and bottom of the mound at Coldrum. The fallen stones can be seen at the bottom of the slope.

Stonehenge *SU123423*

If you ask anyone to name a stone circle, their first answer will almost certainly be Stonehenge in Wiltshire; without doubt, it is the most famous in the world. So much has been written about this megalithic masterpiece that I was almost tempted to leave it out of this book on the grounds that I could not possibly have anything to add. However, some aspects of this familiar site are still enigmatic.

My favourite quirk, due to its downright perversity, is that despite giving rise to the term 'henge', Stonehenge is not a typical henge at all. Classic henges have a ditch inside a raised bank – at Stonehenge the ditch is on the outside. This raises all manner of questions, not

Above: The builders' extraordinary craftsmanship is clear to see on 'Stone 56', the one remaining stone of the Great Trilithon. Without its covering lintel, the tenon joint shows how the trilithons were intricately fitted together. Slightly to the right, notice the gentle curve of the lintel. Below left and right: Other examples of the builders' meticulous workmanship are still visible throughout the site.

just about the function of the ditch, but also the function of the site itself. The best-known research focuses on the astronomical alignments, the careful geometric arrangement of its concentric rings of pits (notably the fifty-six Aubrey holes) and the site's precise position in relation to celestial observation. But as Anthony Johnson observes in his book *Solving Stonehenge*, we can become so overwhelmed by the technical mastery that we lose sight of the people and their motivations.

How many different purposes might Stonehenge have served over its long period of building and development? Was it always an open structure or did it have timber walls and a roof? Why is Stonehenge, with its hanging lintels, so unlike any other megalithic site in Britain? What was the rationale behind the exterior ditch?

Opposite: 'Stone 56' towers over its neighbouring sarsen.
Above: Visible in the centre of the picture, two of the bluestones are dwarfed by the massive trilithons.
Below: In contrast to almost every other megalithic site, Stonehenge seems to be constantly surrounded by visitors.

Amongst the many long-standing mysteries of Stonehenge is one centred on the bluestones. What was so significant about them that they should be brought 132 miles (as the crow flies) from Preseli in south Wales? Perhaps some of the most exciting revelations in recent years have come from excavations by Timothy Darvill and Geoffrey Wainwright in Wales and Wiltshire. First came the discovery in 2004 of the quarry-site at Carn Menyn in Preseli, which actually provided the bluestones. Not far from the site, which is still strewn with discarded monoliths, an oval of bluestones was discovered. In size, shape and arrangement, this bears a remarkably close similarity to that at Stonehenge. It seems almost certain that the two sites were created by the same people.

Then, in 2008, excavations at Stonehenge itself indicated that the bluestone circle was erected between 2400 and 2200 BC, three hundred years later than previously thought. Remarkably, findings also implied that the function of Stonehenge changed too, from a place for the dead to a place for the living. And what's more, a place of healing. Have we found a prehistoric hospital?

Above: The surrounding buildings provide a sense of scale for the Avebury megaliths.
Opposite: Small concrete posts mark the position of other stones, mostly removed and
broken for building work in the eighteenth century.
Below: Looking along the West Kennet Avenue in the direction of Avebury.

Avebury *SU101701*

Chalk. Imagine a land where the ground is full of money, where even your discarded building rubble has value. Essentially, for our ancestors, the chalk geology of Wiltshire was exactly that, because where there is chalk, there is flint. It is unclear whether the land was exploited on an industrial scale, but unworked flint cores from Wiltshire have been found over large areas of the south. Could this be why the whole complex around Avebury and Stonehenge is on such a grand scale? Did the land provide such wealth that communities had the time and resources to dedicate large numbers of people to such extravagance? Avebury includes Britain's largest stone circle, with a henge that is estimated to have required around one and a half million man hours to create. A team of a hundred people would have had to work every day for four and a half years to dig the ditch and bank; and that doesn't even include moving the stones.

The entire Avebury complex is a sprawling affair. To the south of the massive earthwork is the West Kennet Avenue which passes to the east of Silbury Hill.

Many, if not most of its stones are long gone, having been broken and buried, but it has lost none of its sense of grandeur as it approaches Avebury itself. Even in its present, weathered state, the collection of monuments at Avebury is almost an assault on the senses. In its original form it must have been as beautiful as it was ostentatious. The ditch was once sheer sided and over thirty feet deep, with a bank rising twenty feet higher than the central plateau. The gleaming white chalk walls would have made this a show site like no other.

For the visitor to Avebury, it is well worth taking a guided tour of the site, as there is simply too much to take in otherwise. When one also considers that each of the small concrete posts marks the position of other, missing stones and megaliths, a still grander monument becomes apparent.

Above and right: A comparison between the ditch and bank as they appear today and how they may once have looked. (Reconstruction by Michael Bott for the film Standing with Stones.*)*

Above: Modern concrete cylinders mark the concentric rings of wooden posts that once stood at Woodhenge.
Opposite below: The entrance stones of West Kennet long barrow, the largest of its kind in England and Wales.
Below: Silbury Hill, the largest man-made mound in Europe, still dominates the surrounding landscape.

Woodhenge, West Kennet & Silbury Hill
SU151434, SU105678 & SU100685

Continuing the Wiltshire extravaganza, it becomes clear that large-scale construction was not confined to henges and stone circles. Woodhenge, less than two miles northeast of Stonehenge, was a large, circular structure consisting of concentric rings of timber posts and probably roofed. This sophisticated building was set within a circular ditch and bank.

The Neolithic giants of West Kennet long barrow and Silbury Hill, just south of Avebury, were also built to be noticed. West Kennet, some 100 yards in length, is the largest long barrow in England and Wales. Grander still, Silbury Hill is the largest man-made mound in Europe, and, remarkably, was not round as it appears today, but a towering polygonal pyramid; its purpose remains unknown. It has been calculated that it would have taken a team of five hundred men ten years to build. As Julian Cope observed in *The Modern Antiquarian*, with reference to Durrington Walls: 'But who did the catering?'

Above: Stanton Drew's smaller northeast ring. Some of the main circle's stones are visible in the background.
Opposite: The cove at Stanton Drew lies behind the church in the garden of the local pub.
Below: The results of the 1997 magnetometer survey by English Heritage.

Stanton Drew ST600633

Despite its place as Britain's second largest stone circle, today Stanton Drew in Somerset has little more than a bland appearance in the landscape. The site is complex, comprising three stone circles, two avenues, a cove and an outlier, but its vast size and widespread stones have, until recent years, offered little on the surface to generate excitement. However, advances in modern technology have given archaeologists an unprecedented ability to 'see' into the past and Stanton Drew, perhaps more than any other site, has been revealed as the remains of something breathtaking.

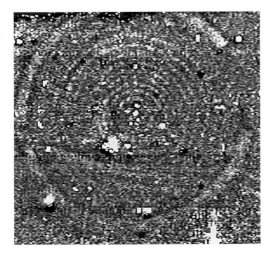

In 1997, the Ancient Monuments Laboratory of English Heritage carried out a magnetometer survey which revealed nine concentric rings of post holes. Each of the holes was three feet or more in diameter and set around the same apart. Equally surprising was the discovery that the circle lay inside a ditch 23 feet wide and roughly 443 feet in diameter. One can only speculate as to the purpose of such a lavish construction, but clearly Stanton Drew was of immense importance and must have been an awe-inspiring sight.

Opposite and below: Wayland's Smithy's imposing forecourt.
Above: The entrance to the main passage, which contains three burial chambers.

Wayland's Smithy *SU281854*

Sitting high on the Cotswold Ridgeway in Oxfordshire, Wayland's Smithy, one of the Severn-Cotswold-style long barrows, underwent distinct phases of development between 3700 and 3390 BC. The imposing stone structure visible today represents the second phase of building and was constructed over an earlier wooden mortuary house. Excavations in 1919 revealed no grave goods, but the main chambers of the later building contained the remains of at least eight individuals. The earlier wooden construction, excavated in the 1960s, was found to have a paved area which was covered in a layer of burial remains eight inches deep. The disarticulated body parts of at least fourteen individuals belonged to this phase, and one complete individual was buried separately to the north end of the paved area.

Perhaps because of Wayland's Smithy's secluded woodland setting, it is one of the most striking long barrows to visit. Although tiny compared to Wiltshire's West Kennet, the imposing entrance stones make the whole place seem even grander in comparison.

Belas Knap & Stoney Littleton *SP021255 & ST735572*

These fine examples of the Severn-Cotswold-style long barrow are so elegantly constructed that it hardly seems possible that they were built over 5,000 years ago. This style of tomb is defined by the mound's trapezoidal shape, often with a recessed court area at the wider end, and chambers built from large stone slabs. The intricate stone walling is in sharp contrast with the huge megalithic façades of Wayland's Smithy and West Kennet, but other than this, the main variation is in the placing of the burials. At Belas Knap in Gloucestershire, chambers are situated in the external walls, whilst at others such as Stoney Littleton in Somerset, the chambers are internal, built into the walls of the central passage.

An interesting feature of Stoney Littleton is a large fossil ammonite to the left of the passage entrance. It is hard to imagine how our Neolithic ancestors related to such things, but here, at least, it was significant enough to be given pride of place by the builders.

Above: The forecourt of Belas Knap in the Cotswolds.
Opposite below: At Stoney Littleton a fossil ammonite was carefully positioned at the tomb's entrance by the builders.
Below: Stoney Littleton in Somerset remains unspoilt and is one of the finest examples of a Severn-Cotswold long barrow.

Rollright Stones

SP296309

On the Cotswold Ridgeway, in the hills south of the village of Long Compton in Oxfordshire, the Neolithic circle of the Rollright Stones seems impressive and weary, in equal measure. Early morning mists give the circle's gnarled stones an otherworldly feel, which fits well with the site's legends of witchcraft and the supernatural. Also called the King's Men, the Rollrights are yet another band of unfortunates, in this case turned to stone by a witch. Although far fewer today, the group was once a tightly packed circle of eighty or more stones.

The King Stone (below), a tall outlier, is separated from the circle by a fairly busy road. Its strange shape is reputedly the result of superstitious travellers over the centuries

Above: The dark trees which hide the circle of gnarled stones from the road, add to the eerie atmosphere of the Rollrights.
Opposite: The forlorn dolmen of the Whispering Knights.
Below: The Rollright circle was once an unbroken ring save for an entrance to the southeast.

chipping away pieces of the stone as lucky charms, which is possible, as the Cotswold Ridgeway is considered to be amongst the oldest trade routes in Britain. In *A Guide to the Stone Circles of Britain, Ireland and Brittany* Aubrey Burl compares the Rollrights to some of the stone circles in the Lake District such as Long Meg and Her Daughters and Sunkenkirk. He suggests that the Rollrights could have been a trading place or depot for Cumbrian stone axes. Across the field, a short walk from the circle, stand the Whispering Knights, the remains of what must be the most forlorn dolmen in Britain. According to legend, these huddled stones were once a group of traitors, conspiring out of earshot of the king.

The name Rollright is a corruption of the original form 'Hrolla Landriht', meaning 'the land belonging to Hrolla'; but other than being the named land owner, nothing else is known about him. The name is also said to derive from a Norman called Roland who fought a battle nearby. Teasingly, there really was a battle close to the circle which took place in AD 916. Sadly though, such is the nature of legend, Roland died in AD 778.

wales & anglesey

Pont y Pridd
Rocking Stone
& Tinkinswood

ST081901 & ST094735

The origins of the bardic traditions are lost in the mists of time and it is this ancient custom of story-telling which connects these two very different sites.

The Rocking Stone was probably left, alone on its high vantage point over the town of Pont y Pridd in south Wales, by glacial movement at the end of the last Ice Age. Reputedly, it has been a meeting place of bards for centuries and such is its enduring importance that the circle surrounding the stone was constructed in the late nineteenth century in honour of its bardic heritage.

Tinkinswood, ten miles south of Pont y Pridd, is another of the Severn-Cotswold long barrows and boasts the largest capstone in Britain, thirty feet long and weighing around forty tons. This Neolithic giant was built nearly

6,000 years ago, and as is usually the case with these tombs, the burial remains were disarticulated. Tinkinswood contained the jumbled bones of some fifty people and it has been suggested that the rituals connected with these burials were less concerned with the individual and more focused on creating an ancestral bone pile.

As for the connection with the Pont y Pridd Rocking Stone, there is a wealth of folklore attached to these ancient sites and legend has it that if you fall asleep at Tinkinswood, you will wake either mad, or as a bard. I'm not sure what that says about bards.

Above: The Pont y Pridd Rocking Stone surrounded by its nineteenth-century stone circle. Opposite and right: The long barrow at Tinkinswood boasts Britain's largest capstone.

Opposite: A tiny row leads to the huge stone of the Maen Mawr. Cerrig Duon's small stones are visible in the background.
Above: As dolmens go, Llech y Tripedd can only be described as petite.
Below: Gors Fawr lies close to the Preseli mountains, from whence the bluestones were carried to Stonehenge.

Cerrig Duon & the Maen Mawr, Llech y Tripedd & Gors Fawr
SN851206, SN101432 & SN135294

The megaliths of southern Wales are generally notable for not being 'mega' at all. A few exceptions do stand out, but whatever they may lack in grandeur, they certainly make up for in variety. In the west of the Brecon Beacons, overlooking the River Tawe, the Maen Mawr, 'Huge Stone', stands in stark contrast to the diminutive ring of Cerrig Duon over which it seems to preside. The site's unusual arrangement includes a row of two even tinier stones which are aligned on the circle. Further west, close to Cardigan Bay on the Pembrokeshire coast, Llech y Tripedd is amongst the smallest of portal dolmens. An incongruously large capstone sits precariously atop three short uprights, long since stripped of any covering earth mound.

More small stones make up the circle of Gors Fawr. Nine miles south of Llech y Tripedd, it lies on flat pastureland close to the Preseli Hills, where the Stonehenge bluestones were quarried. With this in mind, it seems even stranger that monuments in this region are constructed of such unimposing stones.

Pentre Ifan is dramatic in any light, but its appearance today is completely different from how it would originally have looked.

Pentre Ifan SN099370

A few miles southeast of Newport in Pembrokeshire, and a short walk from the small parking area, the enormous portal dolmen of Pentre Ifan is all that remains of a magnificent tomb. Indeed, it would take a very tall person to be able to reach Pentre Ifan's lofty capstone. The whole construction once lay in a now invisible oval pit and the covering earth mound has long since eroded away. When built, the mound itself stretched around 120 feet down the gentle slope of the hill and excavations revealed that it was retained by a dry-stone and timber wall.

For such an imposing structure it seems surprising that very few artifacts, apart from some broken pieces of pottery and worked flints, have been found here. No burial remains have been uncovered by excavations.

An uncommon feature of the site is that the information boards are unusually good and well illustrated. It is worth spending a few minutes with them to help make sense of some easy-to-miss features on the ground.

Above and below: There are spectacular views from Moel ty Uchaf towards the setting sun.
Opposite: The remains of a cist lie in the central depression of Moel ty Uchaf.

Moel ty Uchaf *SJ056372*

In location alone, Moel ty Uchaf in Gwynedd is one of the most dramatic of all cairn circles. Situated high on a hill a mile and a half east of Llandrillo, the views are breathtaking. Like many sites around Britain, the surrounding field boundary walls are full of stones which look as if they came from other structures long since disappeared. Indeed, many of them are considerably larger than the stones which make up the circle. Moel ty Uchaf itself is invisible from lower down the hill and appears quite suddenly when you reach the summit. Despite its grand position, all the site's stones are small; this, however, rather than lessening its grandeur, only seems to add to the circle's elegance.

A deep depression in the centre holds the remains of a cist and there is an outlier to the north-northeast. A little way down the hill to the south lies another cairn, where apparently a quantity of white quartz was recovered, and there are another four possible cists in the surrounding fields.

Moel ty Uchaf is one of those sites which is very hard to leave and I recommend any visitor to wait for the sunset, when the place is simply stunning.

The Druids' Circle
& Ysbyty Cynfyn

SH723747 & SN753790

High on the headland overlooking Conway Bay in Gwynedd, the Druids' Circle is the largest remaining monument of an extensive complex. Many of the other circles, cairns and standing stones are hard to pick out in the landscape, but this ring stands out on the horizon, beautifully placed to view the setting sun. The location of this site was probably significant, as it is situated close to a Neolithic axe factory whose products were extensively distributed throughout northern Wales and parts of England. Although the connection with Druids can only ever be speculative, somewhat poignantly this circle is not far from the Menai Strait, which is where, in AD 60, the Druids made their final, unsuccessful stand against the might of the Roman army. It seems equally possible, however, that this circle's name derives from one of its stones, which looks remarkably like a cloaked and hooded figure facing into the circle.

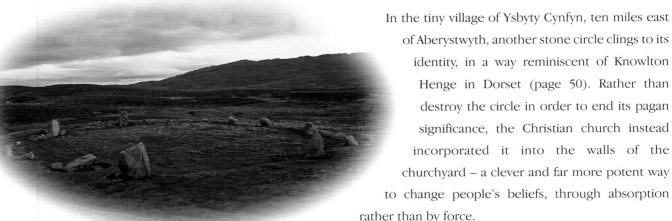

In the tiny village of Ysbyty Cynfyn, ten miles east of Aberystwyth, another stone circle clings to its identity, in a way reminiscent of Knowlton Henge in Dorset (page 50). Rather than destroy the circle in order to end its pagan significance, the Christian church instead incorporated it into the walls of the churchyard – a clever and far more potent way to change people's beliefs, through absorption rather than by force.

Above: One of the stones of the Druids' Circle looks remarkably like a cloaked figure. It actually faces into the circle, but in the fading light seems to be gazing towards the sunset.
Opposite: The Druids' Circle stands close to the site of a Neolithic axe factory.
Right: The stones of the circle of Ysbyty Cynfyn have been absorbed into walls of the churchyard.

Opposite: The massive engraved stone at the entrance to the central chamber at Barclodiad y Gawres.
Above: The stone-lined entrance passageway to the tomb, which from the outside is rather unimposing in the landscape (inset).
Below: Spiral engravings in the eastern burial chamber.

Barclodiad y Gawres SH329707

The late Neolithic passage grave of Barclodiad y Gawres on Anglesey sits high on a promontory overlooking Caenarfon Bay. It is an evocative setting for a site which has given us a rare glimpse into the ritual world of our ancestors. The tomb's passage opens into a domed, cruciform chamber guarded by a huge, intricately engraved monolith. The chamber also contains other smaller stones engraved with zig-zag and spiral designs, bearing a close similarity to passage tombs in Ireland and Brittany. Extraordinarily, excavations in the tomb revealed that a fire had burned in the central area, which contained the remains of fish, mammals and reptiles. Sounding remarkably like a Shakespearean witches' brew, the ingredients were specifically: eel, wrasse, whiting, rabbit, mouse, shrew, snake, frog and toad.

One possible link between all these creatures is that they live in the margins of the natural world: in water, where man may drown; underground, where the dead are buried; or coming out at night, when the veils between living and dead seem to be lifted. It has been suggested that perhaps, to our ancestors, these creatures seemed to pass between the worlds of the dead and the living. But however we interpret this remarkable discovery, the rock engravings alone make Barclodiad y Gawres a rarity amongst passage graves in Britain.

Opposite: *The passage leading to the burial chamber of Bryn Celli Ddu.*
Above: *The western entrance to the mound.*
Below: *Reconstruction by Michael Bott showing the first phase at Bryn Celli Ddu, when the site consisted of a circle-henge.*

Bryn Celli Ddu *SH508702*

Bryn Celli Ddu, 'The Mound in the Dark Grove', experienced huge changes over its long period of usage, and its appearance as reconstructed today is intended to show aspects of different phases. The site was originally constructed as a circle-henge – a stone circle within a raised ditch and bank. This Neolithic open place for the living was later destroyed and replaced by a tomb – an enclosed place for the dead. In this phase, the bank was flattened and the soil used to create a much larger earth mound than we see today. Recent research has uncovered charcoal remains which have been radiocarbon dated, placing occupation at the site back some 9,000 years, making its origins Mesolithic.

During the building of the tomb, stones from the circle were moved, buried or broken. Was this a deliberate destruction of what had been before, or a more careful change of usage, with the elements serving specific purposes in their new placements? Excavations revealed skeletons, cremations and, outside the tomb's entrance, the burial of an ox. One of the more intriguing finds was that outside the tomb, an engraved pillar stood over the ritual burial of an ear bone. This practice is not unknown in prehistoric sites, giving rise to various theories as to its purpose. Could the ears have been placed in this way in the hope that the dead ancestors would be able to hear the prayers of the living?

Above: An engraved stone stood over a burial pit which contained an ear bone.
Opposite: The freestanding monolith in Bryn Celli Ddu's burial chamber.
Below: The monolith's textures resemble split bark, revealing the finer underlying woodgrain.

Another, even more unusual feature of Bryn Celli Ddu is that the burial chamber contains a freestanding monolith, which is essentially cylindrical in shape. Not touching the ceiling, it plays no part in the supporting structure of the tomb. To the builders, the stone was clearly important in its own right. It has been described as 'carefully dressed', meaning that it was cut to be this shape, but close inspection reveals that the surface textures are natural. It could not have been cut to be cylindrical. My immediate impression was that it could be a fossil tree trunk. Its textures are remarkably similar to specimens of fossil wood in my own collection, and I believe this holds a significance which has not previously been suggested. Whether or not this stone is actually a fossil tree may not be important: the relevant characteristic is that it *looks* like wood.

Monoliths in tombs are rare and usually thought to represent a guardian of the dead. Perhaps, however, this stone echoes the strange brew found at Barclodiad y Gawres (page 87), just eleven miles away. To our ancestors, could this have seemed to be something magical which crossed the boundaries of life and death? A thing of life and afterlife? A tree made of stone would most likely have been seen as a profoundly mystical object, with every reason to be placed symbolically in the heart of a tomb.

IRELAND

Castleruddery

S916942

Beneath Castleruddery's weary façade lies a site of remarkable complexity. Thought to be late Neolithic or early Bronze Age, this circle-henge in County Wicklow was once surrounded by a ditch, which was itself surrounded by a further embankment, reinforced by a wall of timber posts. Although no visible traces remain of the outer structures, the stone circle and its bank are still clear to see.

The site seems to be in such a muddle that it is hard to tell whether some of the apparently fallen stones are actually fallen, or were originally intended as recumbents. The entrance is flanked by two enormous white quartz stones, each estimated to weigh around fifteen tons. Dotted around the site are a number of worked stones. One, close to the entrance, matches the slotted stone at Fernworthy on Dartmoor (page 29). Another, drilled and split in an elegant curve, sits outside the circle; the other half of it lies amongst the smaller stones close to the entrance, as if its curving shape held a particular significance.

There is so much to absorb here, and so little of its former scale and sophistication still apparent, that confusion seems inevitable. Castleruddery raises the question so potently: what on earth did they do here?

*Above: The entrance at Castleruddery is flanked
by two enormous blocks of white quartz.
Opposite: A slotted stone like that at
Fernworthy lies close to the entrance.
Right: An elegantly curved stone
sits outside the circle.*

Browne's Hill Dolmen & Poulnabrone

S745768 & M235004

These two portal dolmens illustrate the extremes of megalithic Ireland. Browne's Hill Dolmen (left) in County Carlow bears reputedly the largest capstone in Europe, weighing over 100 tons. The site has never been excavated and one has to wonder whether the builders went to such effort to reflect the importance of their dead, or as a display of strength and ability. Julian Cope has also raised the question whether this colossus was manoeuvred into place by vast numbers of people, or whether it was already naturally in position, requiring the movement of much smaller stones and simpler excavation of the surrounding earth to create the final dolmen?

In stark contrast to Browne's Hill, the elegant portal dolmen of Poulnabrone (below) in County Clare is constructed from sheets of the limestone pavement on which it stands. Dating back to around 4000 BC, it seems to have been in continuous use for centuries and contained the disarticulated bones of at least sixteen adults and six children.

Opposite: The slender stones of Ardgroom look out over the Kenmare River.
Above: The wedge tomb of Labbacallee, or the 'Hag's Bed'.
Below: The circle of Shronebirrane sits beneath Tooth Mountain.

Ardgroom, Shronebirrane & Labbacallee
V707553, V754554 & R772025

Southern Ireland holds many unusual examples of otherwise familiar types of monument, and along the Beara Way the number of megalithic monuments is almost overwhelming. Overlooking the Kenmare River, the circle of Ardgroom comprises stones so tall and slender that it is hard not to imagine it used by equally tall and slender robed figures. This small circle also contains a quirky recumbent stone. While these are normally flat and altar-like, this one is thin and peaked, perhaps deliberately in keeping with its companions.

A few miles to the east, Shronebirrane, another of the recumbent stone circles, stands oppressed in the shadow of the aptly named Tooth Mountain. From the tall portals, the stones reduce in height so sharply to the ground-level recumbent that from the road it could almost be mistaken for a ruined long barrow. A low central mound simply adds to the strangeness of the arrangement.

Further east, near Fermoy, the wedge tomb of Labbacallee is an impressive affair, dating from the late Neolithic/early Bronze Age. Its name translates as the 'Hag's Bed' and, tantalizingly, excavations did uncover a female skeleton, her body buried in the inner chamber and her skull in the larger outer chamber. The tomb is also aligned to be illuminated by the equinoctial setting sun.

Maeve's Cairn & Knocknarea

G625346

County Sligo is home to one of the greatest concentrations of prehistoric monuments in western Europe, and few are greater than the immense Maeve's Cairn. This Neolithic giant is visible for miles around, sitting proudly atop Knocknarea Mountain (below) which dominates the surrounding lowlands.

Dating to around 3000 BC, the thousands of years of erosion can make it hard to imagine how this site once looked. The cairn is enclosed within a wide bank, and the remains of hut circles and other structures lie nearby. Some of these have been excavated, uncovering a variety of artifacts from flints to pottery and axes to arrowheads. Maeve's Cairn itself has never been excavated, but if it can be compared to similar sites in Ireland and Scotland, it is likely that it covers a passage tomb. Whoever does lie beneath this cairn must have been held in the very highest esteem to have been buried at such a site.

Opposite: Knocknarea and Maeve's Cairn dominate the skyline behind Tomb 7.
Above and below: Carrowmore's burial chambers and surrounding boulder circles date to around 4000 BC.

Carrowmore G663337

It is a remarkable statistic that there are over 5,000 recorded archaeological sites in County Sligo. Many of these are not prehistoric, but the numbers of individual types of monument are still staggering. Examples include 91 passage tombs, 111 barrows and 38 wedge tombs, all in less than three percent of Ireland's total area. Perhaps not surprisingly therefore, it is home to one of Europe's most important megalithic cemeteries, Carrowmore. Today, around sixty tombs remain, of which thirty can be visited, but this site may once have held two hundred or more. Knocknarea still dominates the skyline, with Maeve's Cairn clearly visible on its summit. The typical tomb here is a dolmen encircled by boulders. It was originally thought that the tombs were contained within earth mounds or cairns; however, with a total absence of cairn material, it is now generally agreed that these boulder-circles were never covered.

Carrowmore has caused considerable debate in recent years owing to surprisingly early radiocarbon dates. Some of the tombs have been placed in the Mesolithic, constructed around 7,500 years ago. Arguments continue, with charcoal beneath one of the tombs being a possible 9,500 years old. If this date is correct, it shows a remarkable length of potentially unbroken human usage at the site.

Opposite and below: Creevykeel is one of the best-preserved examples of an Irish court cairn.
Above: Beaghmore looks like prehistory for the landscape designer.

Creevykeel & Beaghmore *G721546 & H680842*

Court cairns are a distinctly northern Irish style of tomb and Creevykeel in County Sligo is one of the best preserved examples. These Neolithic structures are characterized by one or more covered cairns accessed from a walled and open courtyard area. Excavations at this and other court cairns suggest that cremations were carried out in the courtyard before the remains were placed within the burial chambers. An intriguing feature at Creevykeel is what appears to be an entrance in the northern wall leading to a small circular structure. This is an early medieval addition used for smelting iron, so whilst there may have been a change of function, this site was still in use over 4,000 years after being built.

One of the most extraordinary sites in the whole of Britain and Ireland is to be found near Cookstown in County Tyrone. Beaghmore is a complex of circles and rows which looks like a Bronze Age exercise in landscape design around earlier Neolithic activity. The site seems to be arranged in four groups: pairs of circles are associated with cairns which have approaching stone rows. The northeast group is alone in having only one circle, but much of the surrounding peat remains unexcavated, so it is possible that more of this beautiful site remains covered.

Above: The questionable external reconstruction of Newgrange.
Opposite: The slot above the door lintel at Newgrange is perfectly aligned to the winter solstice.
Below: Many of the kerbstones at Newgrange are wonderfully engraved.

The Boyne Valley – Newgrange O008746

The Boyne Valley in County Meath holds perhaps the greatest monuments of prehistoric Ireland. Situated in the famous 'Bend' in the River Boyne, Newgrange, Knowth and Dowth form a complex which leaves no doubt as to the skill and sophistication of our Neolithic ancestors. Newgrange has been extensively excavated and restored. The gleaming white quartz façade is actually held in place by a concrete wall and it is quite possible that this design is in fact a 1970s error of judgment. The white quartz covered the ground to the southeast of the mound and was thought to have been a collapsed wall. It is much more likely, however, to have been a white paved area at the tomb's entrance.

Newgrange also contains some spectacular engraved stones, most of them in the kerb at the foot of the mound. Excavations revealed that a number of engraved stones from the kerb and the inner passage had actually been placed with their carved surfaces facing into the mound, and it seems probable that these came from an even earlier structure.

Many ancient monuments are aligned towards solar events, but few display the builders' knowledge and skills so wonderfully as Newgrange. Here, the passage rises gently from the entrance to the cruciform inner chamber. This slope is precisely angled for the sun's light to pass through a carefully positioned slot over the entrance, illuminating the chamber at dawn on the winter solstice. Truly an astonishing feat of accuracy and organization.

The Boyne Valley – Knowth

N994734

The plan of Knowth is quite different from its companion sites in the Boyne Valley. Here, the enormous central mound, built around 5,000 years ago, is surrounded by numerous smaller passage tombs and mounds, some of which are known to pre-date the central tomb. Monoliths (below) and other features from different stages of activity can also be seen around the site. Beneath the great mound there are two passage tombs, one opening to the east, with a cruciform burial chamber, the other to the west, with a simpler, rectilinear chamber.

As with Newgrange, the foot of the mound is defined by kerbstones and here they are nearly all

decorated. It is also apparent from the engravings that some of the stones have been placed upside-down or back to front, again implying that they came from an earlier construction. Amazingly, about seventy percent of Ireland's engraved stones are found in the Boyne region and over a quarter of all the known rock art in Europe is found here at Knowth.

Some designs seem to be simple abstracts, others appear to be much more deliberate and teasingly representational. Stones with simple circles and concentric rings are interspersed with others bearing lavish serpent forms and spirals.

It seems likely that rock art evolved throughout the Neolithic, with designs and motifs gradually coming to relate more to the shape of the stones on which they were engraved. One theory is that the practice changed from having a ritual motivation, where the act of carving was itself more symbolically important, to an increasingly developed and aesthetically based art form. This does seem possible when one compares engravings from the kerbstones at Knowth (right) with the dramatic and intricately planned and later carved stone at the entrance to Newgrange (see page 107).

Perhaps the most exciting aspect of these carvings is that we know many of them were engraved for something even earlier. The fact that they were then incorporated into these later buildings, sometimes with their worked faces hidden in the earth, makes their symbolism and significance to the builders even more of a puzzle.

Opposite: The prettier side of Dowth; the other side has been ravaged by quarrying.
Above: From the top of Dowth, Newgrange gleams in the distance.
Below: Dowth also has a later souterrain.

The Boyne Valley – Dowth O021736

Dowth has not, as yet, been excavated on the same scale as the other Boyne Valley monuments. This passage tomb was once as impressive as Newgrange and Knowth, but sadly the mound has been ravaged by nineteenth-century excavations and quarrying. Some of the engraved kerbstones can still be seen, though the entrances to the two west-facing passage graves are frustratingly closed to visitors. The passages here are shorter than those at Knowth and Newgrange, not extending far into the mound. It is also possible that an indentation on Dowth's eastern edge could be the collapsed entrance to another passage tomb. Confusingly there is also a later souterrain which probably dates to the late Iron Age.

Standing on top of the mound, Newgrange can clearly be seen in the distance to the southwest, hinting of the relationship that these impressive monuments may once have had with each other.

isle of man

Opposite: Note the portal's distinctive shape of a cut, curving stone meeting the straight edge of another.
Above: At Cashtal yn Ard, the row of cists aligns with the forecourt's distinctive portal.
Below: Beyond the row of cists lies a small ritual mound.

Cashtal yn Ard SC463893

The Isle of Man may be a small island, but it holds a wealth of prehistoric sites, many of them quite unusual. Situated in the parish of Maughold in the northeast of the island, Cashtal yn Ard is the best known of all the Manx megalithic monuments, and this Neolithic long barrow is one of the largest of its type in the British Isles. Behind the imposing forecourt, a row of five burial chambers is accessed through a small portal. Curiously, in use, the graves would have made it difficult to pass through the portal for access, which could suggest that this entrance was more symbolic than functional. The portal's distinctive shape of a cut, curving stone meeting the straighter edge of another is not uncommon, but it does seem to have had a particular importance on the Isle of Man.

Beyond the row of graves, aligned with the portal, is a small mound. Excavations revealed that it stood within a burned area, probably for funerary rites. Archaeologists consider this to have been enclosed within a cairn; however, fires in enclosed spaces are uncomfortable affairs and the absence of cairn material makes it possible that this could have been an open space more like an Irish court cairn.

Mull Hill & Arragon Mooar *SC189678 & SC305704*

The Isle of Man's rich variety of monuments extends into the south with two quite different circles. Near the village of Cregneash, Mull Hill (formerly Meayll Hill, meaning 'bare'), is unique in the British Isles and at

around sixty-six feet in diameter, it is the largest megalithic circle on the island. The circle consists of six pairs of burial chambers, each pair

divided by an entrance passage, giving the groups a T-shape. The site has been excavated more thoroughly than most on Man. The chambers contained cremated remains and pieces of pottery, and a number of other items were found, including beads, arrowheads and quartz pebbles. There is thought to have been a cist or chamber beneath the central area, which had been almost totally destroyed by robbing. Aubrey Burl suggests that this was a two-phase monument, where the original central burial became a kerbed cairn with its unusual ring of mini-passage-graves. This conflicts, however, with the findings of excavations in the 1970s.

Above: The circle of Mull Hill is unique in the British Isles.
Opposite below: Each T-shape group at Mull Hill consists of a short passage leading to a pair of burials.
Below: The beautiful cairn circle of Arragon Mooar.

In contrast, the delightful white quartz and granite cairn circle of Arragon Mooar, near Castletown, is tiny. Thought to date from the Bronze Age, there are actually two cairns here, the other being in a ruinous state in the adjacent field. The cairns are in clear sight of each other and would appear to have been associated. From this higher ground, the circle has open views for miles around, with fine weather bringing the mainland into sharp relief. Changing light brings this site alive, but without doubt it is best viewed under a clear moonlit sky.

Opposite: Perched on the cliffs like an eagle's nest, Cronk Karran must be the best situated of all hut circles.
Above: Viewed from the north, the circle's complex layout becomes clearer.
Below: The central pit, invisible for most of the day, is easier to see in the evening light.

Cronk Karran SC192664

To the south of Cregneash, right on the southwestern tip of the island, Cronk Karran must take the prize for the most perfect setting of any circle (see pages 114–15). The area known as the Chasms holds some of the most exciting geology on Man. Millions of years of earth movement have opened narrow fissures hundreds of feet deep and, whilst walking across them is exhilarating, it is really only dangerous to the most careless of walkers. Perched right at the furthest edge of the sheer cliffs, this Neolithic gem is listed uncertainly as both a hut circle and a burial circle. Closer inspection reveals it to be a fairly complex structure. There is a distinct entrance to the southwest beside a thicker section of the western arc. Opposite, the eastern arc is also thicker, with a wide recumbent stone facing the entrance. The longer shadows at sunset make it easier to see the circle's central pit; without excavation, its purpose remains ambiguous. Was this a perfect setting for funerary rituals, a wonderfully secluded meeting place, or simply a peaceful home by the sea? Whichever is correct, there is nowhere else quite like it.

Above: West Baldwin, the site of the Tynwald in 1428.
Opposite: Although modernized, Tynwald Hill in St John's looks every bit a prehistoric mound.
Below: The raised banks either side of the processionary pathway.

The Tynwald *SC277819*

It may seem strange to include two comparatively modern sites here, but the origins of the Isle of Man's Tynwald are lost in the mists of time and may be much older than we imagine. The Isle of Man is home to the world's longest-standing parliament, which celebrated its millennium year in 1979. The name Tynwald comes from the Norse 'Thing Vollr', meaning Parliament or Assembly Field, and the traditional site of Tynwald Hill in the town of St John's is not the only Tynwald in the island's history. A fifteenth-century site, in the hills just south of the West Baldwin Reservoir, is probably the best known after St John's, the circular dry-stone enclosure commanding dramatic views across the lowlands to the south.

What makes Tynwald Hill so worthy of inclusion is its function. The hill, which closely resembles a prehistoric tiered mound, is approached from St John's Church by an avenue 360 feet long which has a raised bank on either side. Every year on Tynwald Day, crowds of people line the banks to watch a procession of the Manx government and officials walk from the church to adopt hierarchichal positions on the tiers, where laws are proclaimed and democratic processes affirmed. The avenue was added to the site in the 1850s, but, evocatively, it looks just like a surviving cursus.

the north

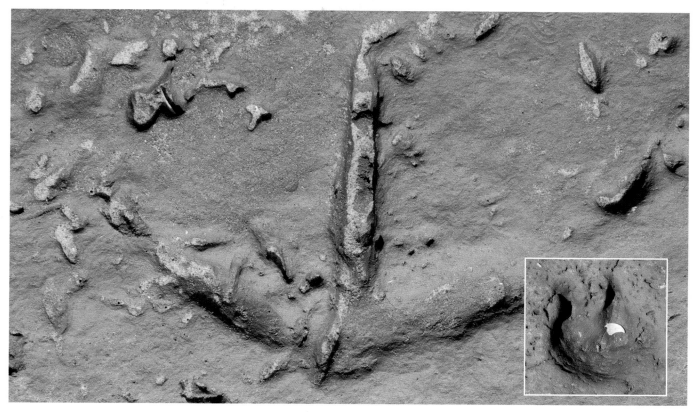

Opposite and below: The male footprints walk away from the camera and then turn back. If you step in the prints themselves, he seems to have been in a slightly crouched walk ... or run, as if running back and forth to catch a Neolithic Frisbee.
Above: Tracks of large birds and aurochs (wild ox) also cover the area.

Formby Point SD270080

Formby Point just north of Liverpool holds a true wonder. All over the world we see structures and artifacts left behind by our ancestors, but rarely do they relate intimately to an individual. Here, the sea has washed away thousands of years of sand, uncovering a 6,000-year-old beach where human footprints and animal tracks have been frozen in time, leaving us a snapshot of Neolithic life.

You can follow the footprints in the main picture, where a man walked towards the water, turned and walked back again. Perhaps he was hunting wild ox, which also left their tracks in the muddy sands. Other animal tracks and children's footprints have been found here too, and it is sad that now they are uncovered, the sea is gradually washing them away. I find it wonderful to think that the man who left these prints could have been one of our earliest builders, out hunting the animals that may have left their tracks on the same day. Or maybe he was just out having fun with his kids. It is the timing of this frozen Neolithic moment which is so magical. Perhaps a day or so earlier and the prints would have been washed away. Even a day later and the ground might have been dry enough for him to have left no trace.

Arbor Low SK160636

This magnificent circle-henge, southwest of Bakewell in Derbyshire, is undoubtedly one of Britain's finest Neolithic monuments. Approaching the site, all that can be seen are the high banks, making the sudden appearance of the central plateau on reaching the entrance all the more exciting. The banks of most henges have weathered to the extent that their height in relation to the central plateau is hard to envisage. Here, despite its erosion, Arbor Low still screams 'SPECTACLE' and reminds us just how impressive these monuments once were. The bank has two entrances, aligned northwest–southeast, with causeways still visible, bridging the ditch. In the centre is what appears to be a cove, where excavations uncovered a human burial. During the Bronze Age, a large round cairn

Looking across Arbor Low towards the northwest entrance.

was built into the bank next to the southeast entrance. This was found to contain cremations and pottery food vessels, but apart from arrowheads and flints, there were few other grave goods.

Perhaps strangely, the flattened stone circle has generated much debate, with opposing views as to whether the stones ever actually were 'standing'. A curious argument, particularly when, as Aubrey Burl has noted, the stones have fallen inwards to the north and outwards to the south, precisely what you would expect with strong northerly winds blowing across this open and sloping landscape. As henges and circle-henges go, Arbor Low is fairly small, but in its way it is every bit as imposing as Avebury.

The Nine Ladies
of Stanton Moor

SK249635

It is always worth the effort to arrive at a site before dawn, and an early morning mist makes it all the more rewarding. Even the most accessible sites seem secluded and remote in a way not possible when the mists have burned away and the sun is higher in the sky.

Southeast of Bakewell, the Nine Ladies stand amidst a large Bronze Age cemetery on Stanton Moor. Over seventy round barrows remain, with a few ring cairns close by. This small circle of small stones is set on a low rubble bank and has the remains of a cairn at its centre. An outlier stands a short distance away to the west-southwest.

Visitors may be confused to discover that the Nine Ladies are now actually the Ten Ladies. A press release by English Heritage in March 2000 announced the newcomer's appearance through soil erosion.

Opposite: At over twenty-five feet tall, the Rudston Monolith is Britain's tallest standing stone.
Above: Concrete posts at Bleasedale Circle mark the original embanked inner timber structure.
Below: A large cist lies hidden in the corner of the graveyard at Rudston's All Saints church.

The Rudston Monolith & Bleasedale Circle
TA098677 & SD577460

In the village of Rudston south of Scarborough, the Rudston Monolith beside All Saints Church is the giant of the British Isles – our tallest monolith, over twenty-five feet in height. As ever, undaunted by hard work, our ancestors brought this huge lump of stone from Cayton, over eleven miles away. This was an important area with no fewer than four long cursuses nearby, now virtually invisible in the landscape, which all converged on the monolith. Another small standing stone and a pair of cists can be found in the corner of the graveyard, brought from ruined barrows in the nineteenth century.

Bleasedale Circle, northwest of Clitheroe, lies hidden amongst the trees which were planted to protect it in the early 1900s. This Bronze Age site is a rare combination of a large outer timber circle and small inner burial mound with a central grave. Today, concrete posts mark the position of an inner timber circle which surrounded the grave. The mound also has a surrounding ditch which was found to have had a floor of birch poles. Like Woodhenge, timber constructions as complex as this remind us that there may once have been thousands of sophisticated wooden structures which have all simply rotted away.

Above: Looking up Pike of Stickle from the site of the Neolithic axe factory.
Opposite: The peak of Pike of Stickle stands proud of the surrounding skyline.
Below: Langdale axes were highly prized and beautifully crafted items.

Langdale Pikes NY275074

A testament to the hardiness of our Neolithic forebears and to their widespread trading, the axe factory in the treacherous crags of Pike of Stickle on Cumbria's Langdale Pikes was heavily exploited for the high quality of its rocks. Axe heads from this spot have been found all across the British Isles, most notably in the east, in Yorkshire and Lincolnshire. The significance of Lincolnshire is its lack of local stone suitable for axe making. Axes would have to be bought. And what price a beautifully crafted axe? A pig? A cow? A pottery urn? There is little doubt that axes of Langdale stone were highly prized items. Some have even been found in burials, unused.

Working stone on the top of a mountain in all weathers, then carrying it down to be finished, would be gruelling enough with modern boots and waterproofs. Now, to a well-prepared walker, bad weather just adds to the adventure, and makes our ancestors' hardiness so much more tangible.

Sunkenkirk

SD172882

Or Swinside, as it is more commonly known. The more evocative name 'Sunkenkirk' is rooted in religious folklore. Versions of the tale vary, but, essentially, a church sank and, as usual, it's the devil's fault.

Little has been done here in the way of excavation, but narrow trenches dug in 1901 did reveal that the site, situated in the southwest of the Lake District, had been carefully levelled in preparation for the circle's construction. A tall, slender stone (second from the left in the photograph) marks the north of the circle. A wide gap on the eastern edge gives the impression of an entrance, but is more likely simply to be the result of missing stones. The actual entrance to the southeast is defined by portal stones (below and far side of main picture).

The farm track approaching Sunkenkirk is on private land and for authorized access only, so it is best to leave vehicles near the road and enjoy the twenty-minute walk to the circle.

Castlerigg

NY291236

Probably the most majestic stone circle of them all, Castlerigg lies high in the hills to the east of Keswick, in Cumbria. Its position, surrounded by mountains, has the atmosphere of a huge natural cathedral, even though it is just as likely to have been a centre for axe trading. It is probably one of our oldest stone circles, dating from around 3200 BC. A wide entrance at the north is flanked by two tall portal stones. A large rectangular arrangement of stones inside the eastern edge of the circle (visible to the right of the main picture and below), was found to contain a charcoal pit but no evidence of burials. I like to think of it as the barbecue area.

I have visited this circle at all times of day, from sunrise to sunset and in sun, rain, mist, snow and howling gales. Whatever the weather, nothing diminishes its grandeur.

Opposite and below: The Druid's Circle of Ulverston has commanding views over Morecambe Bay.
Above: Folklore claims the stones of Long Meg and Her Daughters to be uncountable. Having never arrived at the same number twice, I have to agree.

Druid's Circle of Ulverston & Long Meg
SD292739 & NY571372

To the south of Ulverston in Lancashire, the Druid's Circle, also known as the Druid's Temple of Birkrigg Common, is at first glance a small and uncomplicated site. But an outer concentric ring of low stones quickly becomes apparent, and the complexity of this elegant Bronze Age monument begins to emerge. Excavations revealed that both circles originally stood on a cobble platform. The inner circle, once paved in blueish cobbles, contained a number of cremations.

In total contrast, Long Meg and Her Daughters north of Penrith, is the sixth largest stone circle in Britain. Meg herself is the tall outlier overlooking the circle, and is engraved with a number of rings and spirals. Alignments between Meg and her daughters point to the midwinter sunset. To the northeast is a small circle known as Little Meg, which originally surrounded a barrow containing cremated remains. Long Meg and Her Daughters remains unexcavated, although aerial photography shows a number of structures nearby, possibly pre-dating the circle.

scotland

& the ISLES

Opposite: The stones of Glenquickan seem to be sinking slowly into the damp earth, with one at the southwest just visible in the grass.
Above: Cairnholy's forecourt and burial arrangement are reminiscent of Cashtal yn Ard on the Isle of Man.
Below: The Twelve Apostles of Holywood is the seventh largest stone circle in Britain.

Glenquickan, Cairnholy & the Twelve Apostles
NX509582, NX518539 & NX947794

These three sites in southwest Scotland are a possible witness to a once widely shared culture. Glenquickan in Dumfries and Galloway is, like Boscawen-Un in Cornwall, one of the rare circles to have a large central monolith. Here, the massive granite pillar in the circle's cobbled interior leans slightly to the south. Two other circles, now long gone, used to stand nearby. Three miles to the south, the chambered cairn of Cairnholy has an impressive façade of tall and slender uprights. The narrow entrance opens on to a straight row of burials, very reminiscent of Cashtal yn Ard on the Isle of Man. Its counterpart, another chambered cairn known as Cairnholy 2, lies a short distance away.

A couple of miles northwest of Dumfries, the Twelve Apostles of Holywood is Britain's seventh largest circle after Long Meg and Her Daughters, less than fifty miles away. Considering the possible links with trading, is it coincidence that the Twelve Apostles are, to within ten miles, equidistant between Avebury in Wiltshire and the Ring of Brodgar on Orkney, the first and third largest circles in Britain?

Above and below: Cairnbaan's cup-and-ring markings have a radial groove in each ring. All except one (above centre) seem to point towards the sunrise. Opposite: The huge map-like stone at Achnabreck.

Cairnbaan & Achnabreck

NR839911 & NR856907

Scotland has a wealth of engraved stones and these two sites in the far west near Kilmartin in Argyll are particularly fine examples. Their purpose has always been a subject of debate. Were they maps? Did they represent constellations? Were they of religious or spiritual significance or simply art? There is no way we can be absolutely sure and it is likely that they had more than one function.

An interesting feature of the cup-and-ring markings on one of the stones at Cairnbaan is that they all have a single channel, cut as a radius from the centre. In itself this is not uncommon, but here they all point towards possible sunrise positions, except one which points too far to the south (above centre). Does this mean that the sunrise is irrelevant, or was there a reason to make that one different?

The carvings at Achnabreck really do look like a map. Clusters of small circles sit between larger concentric rings, all interlaced with meandering lines, resembling footpaths between groups of houses. As with most prehistoric art, we'll probably never know their true purpose.

Opposite: The massive cupmarked central stone of the Great X.
Above: Ballymeanoch's row of four stones, cupmarked and graded in height.
Below: Looking north at Nether Largie South Cairn.

Ballymeanoch, the Great X & Nether Largie
NR833963, NR828976 & NR829979

Still close to Kilmartin, another collection of Neolithic monuments is bewildering in its complexity. Ballymeanoch has a row of four tall cupmarked monoliths, graded in height. A short distance away are another two tall stones, set parallel with the larger row, possibly for sighting celestial events. There is also a tiny henge to one side of the field.

Less than a mile to the north, the Great X is a further remarkable group of cupmarked stones. It is thought to have been a lunar observatory, with distinct alignments between the stones and features on the horizon. Stretching in a line through the fields to the north, the cairn cemetery of Nether Largie contains numerous engraved stones.

Seeing these huge cupmarked monoliths so close to the engraved stones at Cairnbaan and Achnabreck raises the question of possible re-use. Is it possible that the carvings were originally created on flat-lying stones and then brought to stand upright in these arrangements long after their original meaning had been forgotten?

Temple Wood

NR827978

J ust across the lane from the Great X, Temple Wood is a site with a complex history. It consists of two circles, a smaller one to the north (visible in the background) and a larger one to the south. Heavy peat covers the valley floor and, remarkably, the larger southern circle would never have been found if archaeologists had not been excavating its partially uncovered partner.

Sometime in the fourth millennium BC, a structure of timber posts was built at the spot where the northern circle now stands. These posts were later replaced by a stone circle, but before this was completed, the builders erected the larger circle to the south. Why they changed their minds remains a mystery. The cairns here date from the Bronze Age – the central one was built around 1300 BC.

It is worth noting the structure of the central cist (below), set within a surrounding circle of small stones in a cobbled floor. Constructed *on* the ground rather than cut into it, this arrangement could make sense of the unusual multiple rings such as Yellowmead in Devon (see page 34), long since robbed of their cairn material.

Leys of Marlee
NO160438

Officially known as Ardblair, this circle is often passed unnoticed by motorists hurtling down this straight stretch of the B947 in Perthshire. It is another fine example of thousands of years of unbroken usage, when a footpath gradually evolves into a progressively busier road. Sometime during the road-building the southernmost stone (below) was broken. The workmen graciously repaired it with concrete and iron bands.

Fortunately there is space to park in a small lane nearby. The ill-placed, ghastly yellow and black warning sign is appropriate. On a busy day the road is as treacherous as the A35 passing Nine Stones in Dorset (see page 49).

The Recumbents – Cothiemuir Wood,
East Aquorthies & Old Keig NJ617198, NJ732208 & NJ597194

Up in the Grampian region of northwest Scotland, the high latitude gave our Neolithic ancestors another way to display their astronomical ingenuity. At fifty-seven degrees north, at the extremes of the lunar cycle lasting 18.61 years, the moon is low enough in the sky to appear to touch the horizon. This union of earth and moon inspired the building of the so-called recumbent stone circles or RSCs. A massive horizontal stone, flanked by uprights, was laid to mirror the horizon so that the moon would appear to float along the 'altar' as it set.

Above: Cothiemuir Wood is perhaps the most beautifully situated of all the recumbent stone circles.
Opposite below: The carefully selected stones of East Aquorthies are a mixture of pinks and greys, flecked with white quartz.
Below: The forty-ton recumbent at the ruined circle of Old Keig was dragged for miles, and uphill, to its resting place.

These three fine examples lie around twenty miles northwest of Aberdeen. Cothiemuir Wood is in a magical setting. Through the trees, the twenty-ton recumbent's relationship to the horizon can just be discerned. A large central block of granite covers a probable burial pit.

East Aquorthies is set within a bank and is unusual in having two enormous blocks supporting the recumbent. The once-majestic circle of Old Keig is now in a ruined state and stifled by farm walls. The vast recumbent weighs around forty tons and its relationship with the landscape is still clear to see.

Opposite and below: Midmar Kirk – rocks of various sizes have been used to wedge the recumbent perfectly in position. Above: Sunhoney's cupmarked recumbent has toppled over, making its relationship with the landscape hard to discern.

The Recumbents – *Midmar Kirk & Sunhoney*

NJ699065 & NJ716057

Twenty miles or so west of Aberdeen, the circle of Midmar Kirk stands amongst the gravestones beside its young upstart church. RSCs normally contain ring cairns or evidence of burials, but nothing remains in this circle, all traces removed by a long succession of tidy gardeners. The flankers arc imposingly, accentuating the focal point of the altar, the accurate placing of which is clear to see. Boulders and smaller stones have been wedged carefully into position to attain a perfectly horizontal surface.

The circle of Sunhoney only a mile to the east, is beautifully situated looking out from its hilltop. The heavily cupmarked recumbent has now toppled over, making it hard to appreciate how it once followed the contours of the landscape. When excavated, Sunhoney's large central ring cairn was found to contain a number of cremated remains. It is now in such a ruined state that it could easily be missed altogether.

The Recumbents – Loanhead of Daviot
& Stonehead *NJ748288 & NJ601287*

Loanhead of Daviot (above), ten miles northwest of Inverurie, is an impressive recumbent stone circle with an adjacent cremation cemetery. Excavations in the 1930s revealed that the circle was built on a levelled platform and its wide ring cairn with open central area (left) was found to contain numerous burials, including skull fragments from young children. The circle's stones also covered small cairns which contained charcoal and pottery fragments. The circular cremation cemetery is thought to have been in use after the stone circle. It contained the remains of over thirty people, including the partially cremated body of a man holding a stone pendant.

Stonehead (opposite), twenty miles to the west, has lost all but its altar and flankers. What makes this RSC so impressive is that the recumbent mirrors the shape of the skyline so perfectly that in twilight, the two seem to merge seamlessly together.

The Grey Cairns of Camster, the Clava Cairns & Corrimony *ND260442, NH383303 & NH758445*

In the far north, not far west of Wick, the Grey Cairns of Camster are as impressive as they are immense. Long wooden walkways meander across the marshy terrain to a small round cairn and the much larger horned long cairn of Camster Long (above). This huge structure was once two separate round cairns, like the smaller one nearby, but they were incorporated into this giant monument some time long after the original structures were built. It is worth the dark, damp and dirty effort to crawl along the long, low and cramped passageways. The silence of the burial chambers is profound.

Above: The immense Grey Cairns of Camster.
Opposite: The northern cairn at Balnuaran of Clava.
Below: The now roofless chamber at Corrimony.

The Clava Cairns, named after the site of Balnuaran of Clava to the east of Inverness, date from the Bronze Age. The site consists of two passage graves and a central ring cairn with radial causeways. It is thought that they were only used for short periods of time and contained few burials, perhaps only one. The surrounding stone circles were later additions, erected when the cairn's use came to an end. To the southwest, Corrimony is another fine example of a cairn, with a large cupmarked stone on top which may have been the original capstone.

Above: Looking east along the western limb.
Opposite: Sunrise from within Callanish's circle.
Below: A chambered tomb lies in the centre of the stone circle.

Callanish NB213330

S ituated on the northwest coast of the Isle of Lewis in the Outer Hebrides, Callanish is undoubtedly the prehistoric jewel of the British Isles. This lavishly complicated monument is more breathtaking than any other site. More like an observatory than a temple, its astronomical alignments far exceed the ingenuity of the recumbent stone circles to the south. Callanish is accurately aligned on the equinoctial sunset and the Pleiades, but its principal focus is the lunar cycle. Here, when the moon reaches its southern extreme and descends to graze the horizon, it seems to appear amongst the stones as it sets.

The cruciform arrangement of richly veined stones aligns with the cardinal points, the short southern row at the top of the cross being the most accurate. At the intersection of the cross, a circle of nineteen stones surrounds a chambered tomb, added centuries after the rest of the site was erected. The northern limb is a long, wide avenue which narrows as it approaches the circle. Notches and angles are cut into many of the stones, creating sightlines in all directions.

There is still much to be learned about the complex alignments of this beautifully elegant monument, and the central circle of nineteen stones raises another question. There are many such circles across Britain and it is generally accepted that these mark the full 18.61-year lunar cycle. The most accurate number of stones to mark half that cycle is nine. Is it possible that many of the nine-stone circles are less accurate versions of the same concept? And are the wider gaps which we so often interpret as entrances, actually deliberate offsets to adjust the unavoidable inaccuracy of the smaller number of stones?

Callanish brings a peaceful stillness whilst also setting the mind racing with ideas. Without pen and paper, just how did our ancestors plan and organize such extraordinary feats of engineering and construction?

Right and below: Most of the stones at Callanish are cut with angles and notches creating sightlines throughout the site.

Opposite: Each wall of the passageway is a single piece of stone twenty-three feet long.
Above: Maes Howe sits on a raised mound which was probably once a circle-henge.
Below: Some fascinating graffiti were left by the Viking tomb robbers.

Maes Howe HY318127

Way up in the north, on the island of Mainland, Orkney, our ancestors were just showing off. The monuments here are bigger and more flamboyant than most others on the whole of mainland Britain. Maes Howe is a magnificent passage grave with a lofty corbelled roof. Like Newgrange (page 106), it is aligned so that the central chamber is illuminated by the sun at winter solstice. Each wall of the passage is constructed of a single, immense piece of stone twenty-three feet long. An astonishing feat in itself.

Unique in Orkney, this mound is set within a circular ditch and bank. Excavations by Colin Richards in the 1990s revealed a number of structures beneath the central plateau, offering the possibility that the tomb was constructed on an earlier circle-henge. An unusual and exciting feature of the chamber is that the walls bear Viking runic inscriptions, which tell of a great treasure, removed from the tomb over three days and nights. If true, another question is raised. What might still lie beneath the unexcavated stones of such giants as Maeve's Cairn in Ireland?

Ring of Brodgar

HY294133

What madness is this? On such a tiny island as Mainland we find the third largest stone circle in Britain after Avebury's outer circle and Stanton Drew. And not just a stone circle, but a massive circle-henge. The henge's wide causeways are still visible, but the outer bank, if it ever had one, has long since eroded away, leaving the enormous stones exposed to the outside world. Fewer than thirty of its original sixty stones remain, and a beautifully lichen-coated outlier (below) stands some way to the west of the ring.

Astronomical alignments at Brodgar are unclear, so its purpose remains a mystery. Its importance however, is in little doubt. This huge site would have demanded an equally huge and skilled workforce. The modern-day mystery is why so many notice boards still refer to these craftsmen simply as 'farmers'.

The Stones of Stenness

HY307125

The improbably tall, blade-like Stones of Stenness, like the nearby Ring of Brodgar, once stood within a henge. This site is indisputably a ruin, but the few remaining stones seem even more extraordinary, set within the much smaller circle than Brodgar. In the centre lies what appears to be a cove with a curiously angled stone nearby. Charcoal from within the ditch and the circle has been dated to the Neolithic period and it is possible that the circle was constructed over an earlier homestead.

The impression here is quite surreal and the sharp angles add to its strangeness. There is still much to be understood, but the Stones of Stenness would be equally at home in a modern art collection.

Above: A view over the houses shows their common design and layout.
Inset: Looking down into the drainage system which runs beneath the village.
Opposite: The view through the low doorway into House 1.
Below: Narrow passageways connect the semi-subterranean houses.

Skara Brae *HY231187*

Skara Brae is, to many, one of the most important sites in the British Isles. But many also miss its true significance. What makes the Orkney Islands unique is that, unlike the rest of Britain, they were never forested. Timber would have been a valuable scarcity reserved for roofing or boat building. When everyone else across Britain was working with wood, here the standard building material was stone.

This Neolithic village was first exposed to modern eyes in 1850 when a great storm ripped away the same protecting sands which had probably ended its occupation. The then Laird removed a number of artifacts and put a window into one of the houses for his daughter, who played there, but no proper excavation took place until the 1920s. The site was occupied for around six hundred years, between 3100 and 2500 BC, dating to the same period as Maes Howe and Stenness five miles to the southeast.

In design, the houses are semi-subterranean, set amongst midden deposits, sheltered from the sea winds and linked by communal passageways. The central living areas are roughly rectangular and at first glance it all seems too modern. With the obvious exception of missing roofs, the houses are almost complete, with cupboards, beds, stone boxes, fireplaces, even dressers and recessed shelves. Even more impressive than this, however, is the presence of a sophisticated underground drainage system and the likelihood that each house had a toilet – something we imagine only arrived with the Romans some thousands of years later. In each house the hearth is centrally placed; either side of it is a stone-lined bed, one slightly larger than the other. It is generally thought that the larger bed was for the men, although the two sizes could also have separated adults and children.

An important point is raised here. Recent excavations of timber structures in southern England have revealed characteristics in common with these stone monuments. What level of sophistication in wooden structures elsewhere has simply rotted away without trace?

Right: The master-bed has its own overhead recessed shelf.
Below: The entrance is to the left of the photograph. The smaller doorway to the right leads to another chamber, probably for storage.

Opposite: The Tomb of the Eagles' entrance is so low that there is only just enough space to crawl through on hands and knees.
Above: One of the tomb's artifacts is a beautifully polished button of albatite.
Below: Burials were placed on ledges and in compartments below them.

Tomb of the Eagles *ND470845*

In 1958, about the same time that my mother was waddling around pregnant with me, Ronald Simison stumbled across a buried section of dry-stone wall on his farm on the Orkney island of South Ronaldsay, which turned out to be one of the most remarkable finds in recent history. When finally excavated, this Neolithic chambered cairn (officially known as Isbister) revealed a previously unknown cult whose burials included white-tailed sea eagles. Carbon dating of the eagle bones in 2006 showed that they were actually interred around 1,000 years after the tomb was built. Clearly a cultural shift had taken place. It is possible that in tearing away flesh from the human dead, the birds were considered an important part in the spirit's passage to the afterlife.

As well as human, animal and eagle remains, many artifacts were recovered from the tomb, including mace and axe heads, jewelry, stone knives and, unusually, a small button of polished albatite. Items so personal are rare. How was the button worn? On what clothing? How many fingers fumbled to put a thread through that hole? We may never know all the facts, but here, as at Skara Brae, the people themselves are almost tangible.

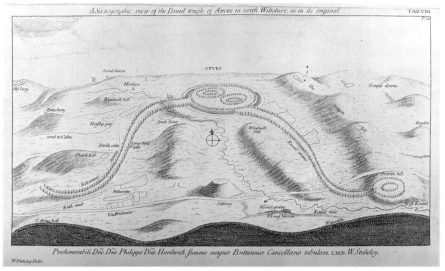

William Stukeley's illustration of Avebury as a serpent-form Druid temple (from Abury, *1743).*

Temple? What Temple?

A huge debt of gratitude can be laid at the feet of our original archaeologists: John Aubrey and William Stukeley, the seventeenth- and eighteenth-century antiquarians who first brought Britain's prehistoric sites to public attention. But along with that gratitude (and this applies mainly to Stukeley) there should also be served a fair degree of blame. Aubrey speculated that Stonehenge was a Druidic temple and this suggestion fuelled in Stukeley an obsession with Druid culture that would dominate his antiquarian work. He adopted the very grandiose title of 'Arch-Druid Cyndonax', and with no shred of evidence considered pretty much every site he visited as of Druid origin. Falling into realms of self-delusion, he often wrote total fiction which he would imply was historical fact. Even his observations fell prey to his imagination. Most notably, despite never having visited Callanish, he copied an earlier illustration showing the beautifully straight stone rows but declared the original artist mistaken. In his eyes it echoed his beliefs about the avenue at Avebury: that it was a gracefully curving, serpent-form Druid temple. In short, he saw what he wanted to see. Once accepted in the public imagination, the idea that all ancient sites were temples stuck fast. Even today, it is the most commonly held belief, and all despite a distinct lack of evidence. Of course, it is quite true that cairns and barrows etc. display a reverence and ritual approach towards the dead. But to apply that as a rule to every stone circle is no more than a triumph of wishful thinking. If future archaeologists excavated an average English country church and adjacent village green with the same set of ideas, they would no doubt interpret the white lines of the local cricket pitch as some sort of processional pathway.

Some years ago, at the end of a long hot day on Dartmoor, I arrived at a pound, an ancient enclosure for livestock, and found that a number of prayer ribbons had been tied in the trees. I will freely admit that I dislike the practice of littering our archaeological heritage, but my feeling was doubled here by the simple case of mistaken identity. This site had heard a lot more mooing than praying. Unlike animal pounds, meeting places have always been multi-purpose. For example, a market square could also have held executions and it is possible that some stone circles served as places of justice. Pursuing that notion, whilst it may be unlikely, it is also possible that burial urns held the remains of criminals, sealed in a vessel to prevent a spirit's passage into the afterlife. Yes, I am being deliberately contentious, but purely for the sake of exploring ideas. Today, our biggest sports arenas can host a football match one day, a rally of Evangelists or Jehovah's Witnesses the next, followed by a series of rock concerts before returning to sport. The only things likely to have evolved significantly are the size of the crowd and, for the West at least, the absence of public executions.

So many of our prehistoric sites have not been excavated, and many that have were excavated a century or more ago when methods were somewhat less than stringent. We have been left groping in the dark to come up with ideas for the social uses of our prehistoric monuments, but with advances in modern technology, especially with the help of geophysics and chemical analysis, more pieces of the immense prehistoric jigsaw puzzle have come to light. The now familiar theory that some stone circles served as meeting places for the trading of axes implies the possibility of more general trading at these locations. If people had to travel reasonable distances to exchange items for precious axes, it is likely that they also carried enough stock to exchange with suppliers of other items, creating an open market for pottery, fabrics, livestock and who knows what else.

Many stone circles and passage graves are known to have astronomical alignments. We can probably never be absolutely certain, but we must also consider the possibility that whilst this aspect was clearly deliberate, it may not have been a significant feature in practical terms. Analogous to this could be the fact that all Christian churches are aligned east–west, a clear reference to the sun's passage through the heavens, yet nowhere within practising Christianity is there any mention of this feature. Cairns, cists and barrows are clearly places for the dead, but the huge variety of sites without a distinct function leaves us with the likelihood that, like our modern arenas, they served many purposes.

I have always been excited by henges, mainly because they have banks and ditches. Unlike most other types of prehistoric monument, henges show a shared practice which demanded man-power and risk-taking on an unprecedented scale. Excavating deep ditches with precipitously steep walls and a frequent risk of collapse could, and probably did, claim many lives.

The Ring of Brodgar's rock-cut ditch measured thirty feet wide and ten feet deep.

We know that the biggest stone circles and henges are fairly evenly spread. Amongst the largest are Avebury in Wiltshire, Stanton Drew in Somerset, Long Meg in Cumbria, the Twelve Apostles in Dumfrieshire and the Ring of Brodgar in Orkney. Even allowing for regional variations, this was a shared culture. There is no dispute that the henges were the mightiest of monuments, and when one considers that the ditches of the Orkney examples were hewn from solid rock as opposed to the more manageable soils further south, it is a fair bet that actually having a henge in the area was important.

Along with the theory that henges were sacred sites and ritual centres, it has long been one of the accepted possibilities that the banks of these enormous monuments were for spectators. It has also been suggested that they could have had acoustic properties which would make it easier for the hypothetical spectators to hear. True, there is no direct evidence but it is widely agreed that their purpose could not have been defensive, as a central plateau within a raised bank would leave those inside as sitting ducks. Similarly, unless there was an army of security guards, the idea that the bank served to obscure the internal goings-on from the public seems unlikely, although it is possible that they did create a symbolic separation between the mundane world outside and whatever spectacles took place inside.

The function of henge ditches has also long been a topic of debate. Were they a further separation between spectator and spectacle, or inner ritual and outer mundane world? Or were they simply a way of supplying material to raise the banks? Realistically, it cannot be the latter. If the purpose was only to provide soil to create the bank, it would clearly be far less arduous to keep lowering the central arena until the amount of soil necessary for the height of the bank had been excavated. It appears that the ditches and banks were of equal importance. Whatever the function, it seems unlikely that a depth of thirty feet or more, as at Avebury, would ever be a necessity. For any of the proposed theories, anything more than ten feet would be excessive, yet frequently we find ditches of fifteen feet or more in depth. It is reasonable to suppose that these ditches shared a common function, but why is there such a huge variation in their dimensions? Shallow and wide, deep and narrow, or multiple ditches where the outer tends to have been shallower and less regular than the inner. Soil analysis at Thornborough has shown that the bank was constructed with the earth from both of its two ditches and the outer ditch seems to have been created with far less care for its appearance. Does this reflect shoddy workmanship? Or was the high level of precision shown inside the henge unnecessary for the purpose of the outer ditch.

Perhaps the answer lies in the underlying geology. If the substrate is consistent and workable, as is the case with the tough but manageable chalk at Avebury for example, a ditch may be dug to any theoretical depth. But if bedrock is close to the surface, it will be far more difficult to excavate the necessary amount of material. In this situation, it would make sense to have shallower and wider ditches, making maximum use of the available topsoil. And what of the double-ditched henges such as Thornborough, Abingdon and Condicote? Interestingly, at Thornborough and Abingdon, the underlying material is gravel; indeed, Abingdon has been virtually destroyed by modern gravel quarrying. In contrast, Condicote rests on shallow clay soils over hard limestone. Is it possible that the double-ditched henges were a practical solution to more difficult working conditions, either because the bedrock was covered by shallow soil, or because, in gravel, a deeper ditch would be unstable and more likely to collapse?

Let's say that a henge is built with a single ditch. The excavated soil is piled up to create seating for spectators. Years pass, the venue becomes more popular and possibly over a long period of usage, the population would also have increased. The easiest and most efficient way to increase the crowd capacity would be, depending on local conditions, either to deepen the existing ditch, or create a second, outside the first, providing the necessary soil to increase the volume of the original bank. If correct, this could certainly explain why so many ditches reached such seemingly unnecessary depths.

Another factor which adds weight to the grandstand theory is the presence of a flat terrace at the foot of the bank, clearly visible at Avebury for example (right) because it forms a level walkway for the audience to move around the circle whilst finding somewhere to sit. Thousands of years of erosion could have removed all evidence of how the banks may have been faced. And were they simple slopes or tiered? It may sound ridiculous to suggest that they could even have been lined with wooden benches, but the five-thousand-year-old stone dressers, benches and recessed shelving at Skara Brae are now known to have been echoed in the wooden houses more recently excavated in Wiltshire. This shows that people's ergonomic thinking at the time was far from primitive.

Excavations can reveal a wealth of physical detail about a site, but in terms of its people, the evidence is far less tangible. What purpose could the ditches actually have served? Theories range from symbolic partitions for religious practices, to their being filled with water. Perhaps by exploring the possible psychology of our Neolithic ancestors we might find some cultural motivations behind their dangerous and labour-intensive extravagance. The remarkable discovery of the concentric timber rings at Stanton Drew revealed such an enormous scale of design and effort that I became obsessed on a Stukeleyesque scale with their purpose. We have no way of telling how tall the posts may have been, but their distribution is almost perfect, suggesting that they were erected at the same time rather than being replacements or reinforcements over different time periods. It is possibly also significant that the rings of posts are so densely packed that if it was a building, the internal space would be almost entirely taken up by its own supports.

For our ancestors, the transition from hunter-gatherer to homestead and domestic farming as a normal way of life was a long one. Neolithic communities may have been relatively large, but back then, farming was more akin to subsistence gardening. Like many indigenous tribal communities remaining in the world today, one of the most important aspects of daily life would have been hunting. It was not until the Bronze Age, when domestic farming was firmly in place, that defending territory grew in importance.

Opposite: The flat terrace is clearly visible at the foot of Avebury's bank.

Parts of Dartmoor remain densely forested, giving a sense of the world inhabited by our ancestors.

Two centuries of Stukeleyism have made many people reluctant to view our ancestors as anything other than fundamentally spiritual. But this view is a luxury afforded by a society which can go shopping for food and never engage itself with the unpleasantness of butchery. To our ancestors it was normal – modern notions of unpleasantness do not apply. The major downside of hunting would be its potential dangers; the risk of counterattack from a wounded and angry animal meant that hunting skill would create status. The most efficient hunter, who regularly came home with a wild boar and without a scratch, would have been admired, respected and probably a regular topic of conversation ... in a land with widespread trading and communication.

Over thousands of years, human understanding has evolved and expanded, but basic psychology has probably changed very little, if at all. Our primary animal instincts remain firm. We fight over the same things and we posture over the same things. Hierarchy is rooted in physical strength and abilities which set an individual or group apart. Gossip and rivalry are a strong combination which allows an exchange of stories on an almost mythical scale. 'Have you heard about the great hunter of the north? He killed twenty boars the size of aurochs in a single day.' The inevitable Chinese whispers spreading from settlement to settlement along trade routes would have fuelled one of man's greatest drivers: competition.

An alternative interpretation of Stanton Drew could offer another possibility. This vast henge contained what we could justifiably call an artificial forest. It is not the only henge known to have contained timber posts, but here there were nine concentric rings of them, each post over three feet wide and set the same distance apart. The thickness of the posts at first seems to imply that they were intended to be tall, but if the banks were for spectators, why build an arena where their view would be obscured? The apparent forest must have been important for the spectacle itself, but if the timber posts were cut to the height of a man, the participants in the spectacle could still be in an enclosed forest whilst leaving the spectators a clearer view over the top from their position on the raised bank. So why create an artificial forest where the spectators could see but the participants could not? As already observed, this was a time when most of the country was still forested and killing animals to feed a family was a major part of daily life. As a consequence, the public display of hunting skill would be an almost inevitable outcome of basic human competitiveness. As well as any number of other possible social events, from rituals to markets, every feature of a henge can be interpreted as a requirement for public displays of bloodsports, and at Stanton Drew, the enclosed artificial forest could have provided a controlled, but nonetheless real, hunting ground. And if these monuments were for bloodsports, without a ditch the animals would easily have escaped up the bank and through the crowd. This could also explain why the ditches were virtually sheer sided and usually too wide to jump. It would take an extremely agile animal to negotiate a near vertical wall.

The superhenge of Durrington Walls in Wiltshire is another site known to have had concentric rings of timber posts. Archaeological excavations here have uncovered animal bones in huge numbers, suggesting that feasting took place on a grand scale. In his book *Hengeworld* Mike Pitts writes in relation to the excavations at Durrington:

The suggestion was that there was so much meat about that a lot remained unconsumed, and flesh still adhered to bones when they were carefully and immediately buried. Further study has revealed the curious fact that some of these pigs (over 95%), domestic – not wild, were apparently killed by archery. The tips of some of the arrowheads are embedded in pig bones. Pigs do not like to die, and make this fact pretty obvious. There must have been some spectacularly noisy and messy occasions in the vicinity of these large timber rings.

Apart from Durrington, the usual lack of animal bones actually found within henges is no surprise. A bull is never butchered in a bullring.

Once domestic farming was fully established, hunting would have become far less important and here we see a potential shift towards the more familiar spectacles of recorded history. With the reduced role of hunting, the Neolithic forested arena could have been cleared to create a Bronze Age open spectacle more akin to bullfighting. The display of courage and strength pitting one man against a massive beast would be a natural progression from a display of skill and agility with food animals. This in turn would have evolved as settlements expanded and territorial skirmishes between tribes became more costly. Our new Bronze Age warriors could display their skills man to man in gladiatorial combat. The first recorded Olympic Games were held in 776 BC, with a fair degree of certainty that they had been established some considerable time before. Also, the Roman gladiatorial spectacles, although later, are known to have their roots in earlier Etruscan religious practices and bloodsports. Where once we wrestled with the natural world, we

Stanton Drew's arrangement of timber posts was revealed in English Heritage's 1997 magnetometer survey. (Reconstruction by Michael Bott for the film Standing with Stones.*)*

ultimately gained such complete control over it that all we had left to wrestle with was each other. Interesting that we still call a wrestling arena a ring, despite the fact that it is square.

Through the thousands of miles travelled in the making of the film and book *Standing with Stones*, my overriding impression was that these were rich and fully-rounded communities. As technology advances, and with it our ability to pick out increasingly subtle clues, we will undoubtedly move to a greater understanding of our ancestors. Maybe they really were the spiritual temple-builders imagined by Stukeley. Or perhaps they were the original creators of all the social structures we recognize from early history onwards. Temples? No doubt. But a functional society needs more. Markets, meeting places, arenas; monuments to watch the heavens, places for the living and others for the dead.

One thing is for sure: in all the known monuments, and those yet to be discovered, our Neolithic and Bronze Age forebears left us a treasure so rich and enthralling that to appreciate it all would take a lifetime. To them we owe our thanks.

Acknowledgments

*For help, support and making a difference,
my grateful thanks go to:*

First, Michael Bott, my friend and partner in making the DVD, *Standing with Stones*, and who created the computer reconstructions in this book. Mike was with me when many of these photographs were taken. In our travels we laughed a lot, researched a lot, walked a lot, drove even further and lived like tramps out of a camper van for months.

Professor Tim Darvill for his invaluable help throughout the writing of this book and setting me straight on a number of things. Adam Sharpe, senior archaeologist at the Cornwall Archaeological Unit, for allowing me to pick his brains and being so generous with his time. Professor John Gale of Bournemouth University for his help on Knowlton Henge. My good friend Stephanie Thurston, who was always ready to do some research for me, usually when I phoned from within the gloom of burial chambers. Dr Andrew Swan, my natural history lecturer at Kingston University, particularly for his help on environmental matters.

Julian Cope, for being an antiquarian inspiration. Writer and broadcaster John Ritchie, for his advice and beyond-the-call-of-duty networking in Scotland.

Landowners too many to mention, but special thanks to Historic Scotland, particularly for allowing me into the houses at Skara Brae. And Kathleen and Freda at the Tomb of the Eagles for trusting me with that button.

My wife, Julie, for always being there and for her tireless proofreading. My father, Henry Lincoln for his enthusiasm, support and more proofreading. My sons, Damien and Alex, who never seem to get bored with what I do (sorry there are no crinoids in here guys!), and Damien in particular, for creating the fabulous website at standingwithstones.com.

Colin Ridler, Sarah Vernon-Hunt, Johanna Neurath, Celia Falconer and the rest of the team at Thames & Hudson, not just for being so very good at what they do, but also for being such a pleasure to work with.

And last but by no means least, for sowing seeds long ago, which have made such a difference to my work: my old art teacher, Bill Randell, and geologist Dr Alan Timms, with whom I enjoyed many enlightening field trips. Both, in very different ways, helped me to reach a better understanding of what my eyes were telling me.

Rupert Soskin

Glossary

Barrow – A raised mound of earth usually over a burial.

Bronze Age – Period from approximately 2200 to 700 BC.

Cairn – A raised pile of stones as a marker or covering a burial. The term is also increasingly used for barrows.

Circle-Henge – A henge containing a stone circle.

Cist – A grave lined with stone slabs.

Court Tomb – A trapezoidal stone cairn incorporating an unroofed internal court.

Cursus – A Neolithic structure consisting of a long straight track flanked by banks and ditches.

Dolmen – A megalithic chamber, sometimes the central structure of a chambered mound.

Henge – Neolithic or Bronze Age earthen circular or oval flat area surrounded by a ditch and outer raised bank.

Hut Circle – The remains of footings of an ancient building, often a substantial circle of stones.

Iron Age – Period from approximately 700 BC to AD 500.

Long Barrow – A Neolithic megalithic tomb containing multiple burials, sometimes with dry-stone walls and covered with an elongated earth mound.

Mesolithic – Middle Stone Age. Period from approximately 10,000 to 4500 BC.

Neolithic – New Stone Age. Period from approximately 4500 to 2200 BC.

Passage Grave – A megalithic burial structure consisting of a passageway leading to a burial chamber.

Severn-Cotswold Barrows – A distinct style of long barrow with burial chambers constructed from massive stones.

Trilithon – Two upright megaliths with a third resting horizontally on top.

Tumulus – A prehistoric mound or barrow.

Wedge Tomb – Late Neolithic style of tomb usually on higher ground, with an entrance at the wider end.

Further Reading

Burl, A., 1976. *The Stone Circles of the British Isles*. New Haven & London: Yale University Press.

Burl, A., 1989. *The Stonehenge People*. London: Barrie & Jenkins.

Burl, A., 1999. *Great Stone Circles: Fables, Fictions, Facts*. New Haven & London: Yale University Press.

Burl, A., 2000. *The Stone Circles of Britain, Ireland and Brittany*. New Haven & London: Yale University Press.

Burl, A., 2005. *A Guide to the Stone Circles of Britain, Ireland and Brittany* (rev. ed.). New Haven & London: Yale University Press.

Burl, A. & Piper, E., 1979. *Rings of Stone: The Prehistoric Stone Circles of Britain and Ireland*. London: Frances Lincoln Publishers; New Haven: Ticknor & Fields.

Castleden, R., 1990. *The Stonehenge People: An Exploration of Life in Neolithic Britain 4700–2000 BC*. London & New York: Routledge.

Chippindale, C., 2004. *Stonehenge Complete* (3rd ed.). London & New York: Thames & Hudson.

Clark, G., 1962. *Prehistoric England* (rev. ed.). London: Batsford.

Cope, J., 1998. *The Modern Antiquarian: A Pre-Millennium Odyssey through Megalithic Britain*. London: Thorsons.

Cope, J., 2004. *The Megalithic European: The 21st Century Traveller in Prehistoric Europe*. London: Element.

Darvill, T., 1988. *Ancient Britain*. Basingstoke: The Automobile Association.

Darvill, T., 1996, *Prehistoric Britain*. London & New York: Routledge.

Darvill, T., 2007, *Stonehenge: The Biography of a Landscape*. Stroud: Tempus.

Hadingham, E., 1975. *Circles and Standing Stones*. New York: Walker; London: Heinemann.

Hawkes, J., 1978. *A Guide to the Prehistoric and Roman Monuments in England and Wales* (rev. ed.). London: Sphere.

Hawkins, G., 1971. *Stonehenge Decoded*. London: Collins.

Hedges, J. W., 2000. *Tomb of the Eagles: A Window on Stone Age Tribal Britain*. Oxford: John & Erica Hedges Ltd.

Hitching, F., 1977. *Earth Magic*. London: Pan Books.

Johnson, A., 2008. *Solving Stonehenge, The New Key to an Ancient Enigma*. London & New York: Thames & Hudson.

Lewis-Williams, D. and Pearce, D., 2005. *Inside the Neolithic Mind: Consciousness, Cosmos and the Realm of the Gods*. London & New York: Thames & Hudson.

Mackie, E., 1977. *The Megalith Builders*. Oxford: Phaidon.

Malone. C., 2001. *Neolithic Britain and Ireland*. Stroud: Tempus.

Miles, D., 2005. *The Tribes of Britain*. London: Weidenfeld & Nicolson.

Mithen, S., 1996. *The Prehistory of the Mind: A Search for the Origins of Art, Religion and Science*. London & New York: Thames & Hudson.

North, J., 1997. *Stonehenge: A New Interpretation of Prehistoric Man and the Cosmos*. New York & London: Free Press.

O'Kelly, M. J., 1988. *Newgrange: Archaeology, Art & Legend*. London & New York: Thames & Hudson.

Pitts, M., 2000. *Hengeworld* (rev. ed.). London: Arrow.

Pryor, F., 2002. *Seahenge, A Quest for Life and Death in Bronze Age Britain* (new ed.). London: HarperCollins.

Pryor, F., 2004. *Britain BC: Life in Britain and Ireland Before the Romans*. London: Harper Perennial.

Renfrew, C. and Bahn, P., 2008. *Archaeology: Theories, Methods and Practice* (5th ed.). London & New York: Thames & Hudson.

Scarre, C., 2007. *The Megalithic Monuments of Britain and Ireland*. London & New York: Thames & Hudson.

Thomas, J., 1999. *Understanding the Neolithic*. London: Routledge.

Thomas, N., 1977. *Guide to Prehistoric England*. London: Batsford.

Useful Websites

For more Standing with Stones   www.standingwithstones.com
Julian Cope's vast antiquarian resource   www.themodernantiquarian.com
Council for British Archaeology   www.britarch.ac.uk
Archaeology Data Service, University of York   http://ads.ahds.ac.uk

Index